T0208260

Leading While Limping

Santarvis Brown

authorHOUSE®

AuthorHouse™
1663 Liberty Drive
Bloomington, IN 47403
www.authorhouse.com
Phone: 833-262-8899

Published by AuthorHouse 03/06/2023

ISBN: 979-8-8230-0284-4 (sc)
ISBN: 979-8-8230-0282-0 (hc)
ISBN: 979-8-8230-0283-7 (e)

Library of Congress Control Number: 2023904508

Print information available on the last page.

Contents

Introduction

Who can honestly say that they've never found themselves telling their peers how they "love" their leader, and then almost immediately following that statement up with a negative trait their leader possess: "I love their leadership, but they're highly inflexible...they refuse to deviate from the book even when it's necessary...they're constantly requesting progress reports?"

Does this sound like one of the leaders you've encountered in your life or like your current leader? Of course, it does!

Whether you like it or not there's nothing unusual about your leader having imperfections or inadequacies, **they're only human**. Being a great leader isn't determined through flawlessness. What makes a leader great is having a firm grasp of personal hang-ups, personal and professional issues, and inadequacies that influences their leadership methods.

Leaders who are great are those who've established how to lead with a limp.

Leading While Limping

Before you'll be able to fully comprehend the concept of leading with a limp, you'll have to learn how to distinguish the difference between authentic and artificial leadership.

These two terms may have set off an automatic reaction and you're probably finding yourself already associating artificial leadership with something undesirable; however, this is incorrect.

Artificial leadership is not necessarily a bad or obstructive way of leading, it's simply a method of leading that is not your own, so it's considered unnatural or stilted. Perhaps you've tailored your leadership to match advice from a colleague or a book you read but this only means that you'll be facing a great deal of challenges. The challenges you face may lead to notable struggles as you preoccupy yourself with the task of concealing your unique, personal leadership skills.

Authentic leadership, on the other hand, offers you the freedom to embrace your struggles and remanufacture them as tools to help empower those who look to you for guidance and who may be facing similar challenges.

Let's say you're a leader and are expected to speak publicly. This means you'd be standing in front of a large group or your team, presenting and sharing information and data. Now, if you're terrified of speaking publicly, this leadership requirement would be quite a daunting task and the 'artificial' leader will convince themselves to push through no matter how nervous or uncomfortable they are—likely stammering throughout the entire presentation.

Authentic leaders, however, lay it all out there. They have no problem admitting to the entire audience that public speaking is not one of their strongest characteristics. An authentic leader may even start their presentation with a joke about how the audience can anticipate

hakiness in his voice or stuttering and mispronunciations—attributed
o the anxiety of being the center of attention.

Instead of viewing the admittance of imperfection as a weakness,
:he audience may laugh and warm up quicker to him since he has shown
:hat just like everyone else, he struggles with certain aspects of his field.
It simply makes him more relatable and genuine which is much more
appealing than pretending to have everything under control or being
above error. Such leadership encourages subordinates to embrace their
flaws because no-one is exempt from them.

It's referred to as *leading with a limp*—identifying and acknowledging
your shortcomings and transforming them into a useful leadership tool.

What Are the Benefits of Leading With a Limp?

Leading with a limp can be beneficial in a number of ways since
the environment you're creating through accepting and sharing your
personal inadequacies motivates your subordinates to follow suit. It also
promotes a healthy team-centric atmosphere and highlights your own
humanity, alleviating some of the pressure you feel as a result of being
held to unrealistic standards.

This in turn, allows your team to openly recognize and welcome
their own struggles–improving your team's support system because not
only do they know what their weaknesses are, but they can also freely
request assistance or advice from a team member better suited in that
specific area.

Chapter 1

Appreciation of the Limp

Executives entering a new job often feel like they're imposters. Research conducted by Harvard Business Review (Carucci, 2015) with thousands of leaders, revealed that 69% stepping into more significant roles feel ineligible for the new roles, and 45% had only a basic idea of the kind of challenges they'd be faced with. A whopping 76% advised that the organizations did not do much to prepare them for their new positions. This notion of being an imposter and pressure of assuming a role you've not adequately been prepared for leads to overcompensation by attempting to be faultless.

Three of the more common, yet incorrect, beliefs are (Carucci, 2015):

"I have to be 100% fair."

Leaders are oftentimes overly and unfairly analyzed when it comes to resource allocation strategies. This refers to the criteria they have for promotions and compensation. Most of the time the uncertain economy and substantial gap between executive and worker incomes are the driving factor behind the lack of trust workers feel toward executives. Meaning employees already anticipate being overlooked for promotions, pay increases, performance evaluations, and new opportunities. Unfortunately, some worker's distrust lacks facts and is inspired by unrealistic expectations from leaders. It's easier for leaders who suffer from the imposter syndrome to fall into this trap and obsess over ways to conciliate this issue.

Yes, it's important to understand that people want to be treated equally, however, it's also important to note that not all jobs and not every contribution holds equal value. Make it clear that rewards, resources, and opportunities are dependent on their proportionate performances. An employee working in a part of the business that requires less knowledge or experience cannot expect to receive the same reward or opportunities as someone working in the more intricate functionalities of the business. This simply isn't fair and making this clear to your employees is easier than you may think since people instinctively know that everyone is not the same. Trying to neutralize these differences by the creation of a false sense of egalitarian approaches will only provoke anxiety and criticism.

Those who look to followers want to know exactly what the rules are and know that leaders are interested in the rules being adhered to. Once employees understand what the standards are and how rewards will be administered, they will be confident that there'll be no mercuriality present. They need assurance that if they fulfill their roles, they will be supported by their leaders irrespective of organizational injustice.

"I have to be perfect."

Many executives refuse to accept that they are human and a part of being human means that they too can have flaws and make mistakes. Your role and responsibilities didn't somehow transform you into an

ll-knowing being that has absolutely no imperfections and has answers
o every single question you are met with. Acting as though you're above
error eventually leads to the expectation of others to be above error.
This is particularly dangerous as it provokes rebellion and causes those
who follow you to withdraw their support. Additionally, it places you
at the center of scrutiny where followers are eagerly waiting on even the
slightest slip-up from you, as to highlight your hypocrisy. It then leaves
the executive terrified of exposure or criticism which causes them to
work tirelessly to preserve the mirage of infallibility—imprisoning them
in the perpetuation of perfection.

Followers need affirmation that those leading know that they
themselves are not exempt from flaws and because of this will be
understanding of the flaws of others. A good leader is open about what
followers can expect from their strengths as well as their weaknesses.
Owning one's imperfections builds trust because a leader's most notable
source of credibility is their vulnerability. Therefore, a leader who accepts
and acknowledges their own weaknesses, encourages others to do the
same rather than hide it and possibly worsen the situation.

"I have to be accessible 24/7."

A never-ending cycle has to be the one where leaders feel they don't
have enough time to give and followers feel they don't get enough
time. The challenge is not necessarily finding the time to personally
interact with those you lead but rather negotiating with each person
what their needs are and how to provide it. It's important to be
available when needed, yes, but offering unlimited access to you could
be counterintuitive and may burn you out. Your responsibility isn't
to provide all the answers at the snap of a finger, your responsibility
is to enforce the need and desire to work within your followers and
equip them with the skills needed to do so efficiently; even when

you're not around. Set clear boundaries and maximize the impact your contribution to creative processes have on the team's success rather than allowing them the luxury of relying solely on your input and presence. Satisfying your team's pressing and genuine needs is more important than trying to assimilate something you could never be.

Difference Between Managing and Leading

People all view the role of a "manager" and "leader" in different ways. The definitions are often misinterpreted and as such, the attitude of each person in that role differentiates. In general, leaders are superiors in an organization who place the company's best interest first whereas a manager is someone who oversees a specific department within that organization. The confusion is taken a step further with the introduction of various named-hierarchies in leadership levels, such as foreman, supervisor, team leader, first-line managers, and so on.

The nature of your title is sometimes dependent on the terminology used by the company you work for—you may be a manager at one organization and a supervisor at another. This, of course, just adds to the confusion because it may leave you with the impression that the one role is more authoritarian than the other. Realistically speaking though, companies tend to change title names in an effort to build morale and support, as to develop a new and improved working environment. It seldomly works, in fact saying it never works may be a more appropriate analysis. Low morale within a company is not due to titles or title alterations—management is the cause of most problems.

Now, let's take a closer look at the true difference between management and leadership.

The Manager

Irrespective of the title given on the hierarchical level of a person, people typically associate a manager's responsibility with managing something-it could be a certain number or team of people within a business, a specific shift, or department. No matter what that something is, a manager's role extends only as far as that specific group of people or nature of activities in a certain area, and there's nothing wrong with that. Although a manager's success is measured purely on how they perform over the department or group they manage; they could be unfriendly or utterly unpleasant but if they achieve their benchmarks in the designated areas, they are regarded as exceptional and successful.

In an instance where a 1st and 2nd shift manager are performing exceptionally, but the 3rd shift manager is battling to hit their metrics, does it indicate poor performance on the 3rd shift manager's part? If your answer is yes, then you share the opinions of many companies who'd replace that 3rd shift manager. I, on the other hand, would contend that the 2nd shift manager is likely the one performing poorly as they have not equipped the 3rd shift manager for success. Additionally, the 1st shift manager is the one benefitting from the skills of the 3rd shift manager, since they set the 1st shift manager up for success.

How do I know this is the case? Well, that's an easy one—the 3rd shift manager is clearly the leader among these three people since their responsibility is to develop ways to improve the business as a whole and maximize overall success. This is where the difference lies. Though the 3rd shift manager is in the same role, they view their role from a broader perspective. This person doesn't view being a manager as managing a shift, team, or department; they view being a manager as a person who helps others accomplish success regardless of being dealt a difficult hand.

All over the world, companies struggle due to perpetuating the ideals of managers, rather than that of leaders.

Transforming a Manager Into a Leader

As explained in the above section, a title doesn't make a leader. If anything, a title may diminish a leader's role. It's common in the workplace to hear people talking about how horrible management is, yet they love their leader–this tends to be a result of a subconscious separation people make between their own leader and the company's remaining management team. This is because good leaders display characteristics that employees consider successful and admirable.

A good leader (Brown, 2022):

- **Is humble and gives others recognition**. Good leaders understand that their success relies on the success of their employees. Recognition of the achievements, actions, and suggestions of colleagues and employees, instills a sense of appreciation and esteem in them. Consider the example of the 1st and 3rd shift managers, if the 1st shift manager publicly acknowledged that their success mainly depends on the efforts of the 3rd shift manager, it could've greatly impacted that shift manager's performance and attitude toward their duties.
- **Listens**. Leading isn't about ordering people around; it's about paying attention and guiding your team to success. Closing your mouth and listening is how you show someone that you respect them and what they have to say. With that said, a good listener doesn't only listen to the opinions and feedback of their own team, they examine the whole picture to determine how their team can improve the company as a whole.

– **Demonstrates the importance of supporting each other.** Once again, I would like to take you back to the earlier shift manager example. The 3ʳᵈ shift manager showed his team what it meant to set others up for success as well as how to do it. Many times, that involves placing your personal metrics in the backseat in order to improve the team's overall metrics. Applying this method usually means the manager receives the least recognition, however, it's likely the most straightforward and effective way to better the whole company. At face value, distinguishing a leader from a manager seems clear-cut, except the implementation is inordinately tasking. Firstly, a leader needs to dispose of the dark cloud that is "ego," because a leader is required to put their personal interests aside and prioritize the interests of the unit. Picture going above and beyond to help everyone else and receiving nothing in return—if you're able to do that, then you already have the basis of what it takes to be an exceptional leader.

Tips to Help Leaders Be Content With Not Having All the Answers

As mentioned before, the role of a leader is to guide and inspire your team. Though you are frequently consulted for insights, you're not perfect which means you won't always have all the answers to every problem or question—recognize that this is okay. The accountability you feel for your team sometimes makes this a difficult pill to swallow, thankfully, members of Forbes Coaches Council were more than happy to share some advice on how leaders can learn to be content with this fallibility (Forbes Coaches Council, 2020).

And here they are (Forbes Coaches Council, 2020):

1. Surround yourself with people who know everything—And no, this doesn't mean one person should know everything you don't know. This means interacting with the people who have detailed knowledge on various things regarding the business. It usually takes a team or group of people to complete the full set of knowledge required and a great leader knows that if they want to absorb that knowledge, those are the people to surround themselves with. Thus, admitting that you as a leader don't have all the answers and turning to your team for assistance indicates a level of respect toward them and their area of expertise. It also signifies that you know how to detect and nurture talent.

2. Be a constant learner—This may very well be one of the greatest attributes a leader can have. The concept of being a lifelong learner allows you to welcome the reality that you won't have all the answers and open you up to seeking help from the collective knowledge of your team members. In turn, you're showing them that leaders are not all-knowing, they just know how to leverage the knowledge at their disposal and should have humility. This partnership or collaboration builds their confidence and will surely boost their performance.

3. Inspire answers by asking more questions—Managers and bosses are the ones who tend to provide answers for everything. Asking questions is something true leaders do and it motivates those who have questions of their own to seek answers. You don't have to have the answers all the time and there's nothing wrong with including them in finding the relevant answer. Even if you do have the answer, respond in a manner that suggests that you would like to know what they think about it.

4. Be the paragon of what you expect from others—A leadership moment is certainly the moment that you admit you don't immediately have the answer being sought. This is what you expect from your team so you should role model that behavior. Be honest, open and dignified about what you don't know— vulnerability is a gift. It makes you more approachable and your team would be more enthusiastic and eager to share creativity and ideas.

5. Plan for various scenarios and weigh your options—The number 1 challenge in leadership is exercising judgment and making decisions in the face of precariousness. Rather than stressing focus on "the answer," teach your team how to pilot the unknowns. Conduct a session with your team for scenario-planning and the weighing of different options. It'll not only enhance your muscle for adaptive leadership, but also theirs. Highlight the non-negotiables and ascertain the rest from there.

6. Develop a growth mentally—A tolerance for uncertainty is rapidly becoming a requirement for leaders in the everchanging working world. Possessing the belief that intelligence can be developed is a major advantage in the modern workplace. The key is to listen and think from a place of inquisitiveness and determination. Ambiguity should be viewed as an opportunity to learn, grow and expand your capabilities.

7. Hand work back to your team—Getting distracted by all the expectations and pressure on people in positions of authority is easy and could leave you feeling disoriented. Taking some time out on the balcony often helps the thoughts flow clearer into your head. You need to know when it's time to hand work back to your team members, and don't allow yourself to feel despondent because of this—it serves as a strength. Once

again, vulnerability is a gift and your team will be pleased to know that you feel like you can trust and rely on them for assistance.

8. Use these moments to build trust—Comfortability in knowing that you won't always have all the answers is essentially a trust-building exercise between you and your team. Building trust is a lot easier when you hire people who you don't mind learning from and depending on when needed, as opposed to hiring people you know can do the work, but you lack the trust.

Chapter 2

Leading Self and Others

The act of leading a group of people toward improvement and prosperity is considered an intricate science and a form of art. The scientific aspect of it relates to a leader's analytical and organizational expertise that allows them to assess people, their potential, and utilize their findings to design and improve the workplace. The artistic aspect of it pertains to the creative and innovative skills a leader possesses, allowing them to effectively conjure ideas, communicate with their team, and adequately implement their conceptions.

Recent years have urged many people to seek guidance on how to improve their leadership skills or how to adopt the necessary qualities for exceptional leadership. Numerous books and articles have been published with tips and tricks on how to become a great leader yet the emphasis is often only on how to lead others; disregarding or understating the importance of the fundamentals required.

An appreciable leader is one who understands the requisite of being able to lead themselves.

The journey to efficient leadership is one that starts from within. It requires a considerable amount of continuous self-reflection, self-awareness, and the capacity to be ever-evolving. Howard Thurman; a philosopher, author, educator, civil rights leader, and theologian, made a statement implying that the lack of knowledge about oneself significantly handicaps one from leading others. It's essential for a leader to have a sense of their own identity before they can develop a constructive and influential style of leadership that compliments who they are.

Now begs the question: How does one discover one's inner-self? Here are 3 methods you may want to implement (Brown, 2021):

- **Recognition of room for improvement and accepting restrictions in your abilities**—no single person can do every single thing so accepting that your abilities may have certain limitations is part of becoming a better version of yourself and a better leader. Denying the fact that you too have limitations will only hinder your chances of growing and learning from them. Understand that limitations are not unchangeable; you may have to work much harder to overcome them and reshape them into a strength over time.

- **Self-reflection**—is exactly what it sounds like; the capacity to assess your actions, decisions, feelings, strengths, and weaknesses. During this time, you open yourself fully to improvement on tasks you know you're not as impressive at and you allow yourself to appreciate the ones you're already spectacular at. Keep reminding yourself of the importance of learning from your positive attributes and not only from your challenges.

- **Continual enthusiasm to improve**—a quality present in leaders who exercise self-awareness. The fact that we can make resolutions with every passing year indicates that we are capable of recognizing a need for change within ourselves and our habits, however, what sets us apart from those who succeed is the perseverance and steadfastness to stick with whatever beneficial alterations we've made to ourselves or our lives. A leader capable of leading themself is not only accountable for their own actions but also that of their teams and possess the tools needed to efficiently self-manage and accomplish goals with adaptability and resilience.

Start by Leading Yourself

While we now know that it's near impossible to successfully lead others until you've mastered leading yourself, many might not exactly understand what this means or entails. The president of The Positivity Project and coauthor of Lead Yourself First: Inspiring Leadership Through Solitude, Mike Erwin—also a former 13-year army officer—provided some insight on what leading yourself really means. Below are some of the key takeaways (Boss, 2017).

Make yourself a priority: Scheduling time to reflect is imperative for your mental wellbeing and brain functionality. As much as your body needs rest after laborious physical exercise, your mind needs rest after mental strain and exercise. Taking time out for solitude allows you to rejuvenate by offering a quiet space to clear your mind and collect your thoughts, in the order you want. People tend to get a bit on edge when you repeat this to them as it has been said so many times by various life coaches and leaders, but that's because it's so true. The majority of personal insights come to you when you're away from whatever is preoccupying you. Taking a step away from the problem you're faced with provides you with a broader view as opposed to constantly viewing it from a micro-level—highlighting the puzzle as a whole and helping you establish which pieces need to go where, as opposed to endlessly staring at that one troubling piece. As Erwin explains in his book, solitude is "a subjective state of mind," that offers one's mind the opportunity to resolve problems on its own, without the interference or input of other minds. Solitude doesn't necessarily mean you're going into isolation, cutting yourself off from the rest of the world. It refers to any extended periods of time you spend in your own company, like when you go for a run or take a shower, to gather all of your thoughts and achieve mental congruence. Taking time to yourself doesn't mean you're antisocial or avoiding people close to you, it merely means you're prioritizing the importance of resetting your thoughts and recovering from mental fatigue.

Solitude provides lucidity, and lucidity offers meaning.

Listen carefully: Listening intently to what your body is telling you is one of the many challenges when it comes to solitude. During the course of the day, you may hear your body telling you things like your back is aching or your mind is screaming for someone to make a decision during a meeting, but the question here is what action do you take in response to it? There may be various things holding you back from performing to your full potential but you're just not listening carefully enough. Are you someone who simply forgets those disturbances and responses until the next moment it occurs, or are you the kind of person who'll take action and address whatever is causing you to be distracted? Listening carefully to everything your body and mind is telling you helps formulate ways to effectively respond to the root cause behind that reaction. If your efficiency is negatively impacted by feeling annoyed that you're frequently being interrupted while working, the appropriate action would be to schedule time for work when there'll be no-one around to interrupt you.

That is the objective of listening and then responding.

Get used to it: Solitude is commonly mistaken for a selfish act because you have things expected of you, people who rely on you, and failure to fulfill these responsibilities means that you're letting them all down. This couldn't be more incorrect. If your team is incapable of functioning without you or competently accomplish work goals, then what does this indicate about the quality of your leadership?

You have nurtured a team that has no ability to remain productive even in your absence—this is not a good impression on your success in developing future leaders.

Leverage mentorship: Neither a mentor or coach has the ability to think of every possible alternative for every situation by themselves. Growth only occurs when a person's perspective is challenged—an issue can't be resolved by the mind which instigated it initially (a little tribute to Einstein's original quote "you can't solve a problem with the same thinking that instigated that problem in the first place"). Having a mentor, even as a leader, means you have guidance when facing crossroads. Your mentor can offer you advice on how they overcame their own obstacles which may have been similar to what you are facing. This doesn't mean you have to or will do precisely as they did, but it opens your mind to a new way of perceiving the problem or solution— helping you draw your own conclusions. Another important distinction to recognize is the manner in which you make decisions. Ask yourself: Do I listen to other people's input and reach my own conclusions? Or, do I use their input to make my decisions?

This requires listening to your own intent before you can make the necessary changes to lead.

Purposefulness: A Pillar in Self-Leadership

Self-leadership and leadership share many of the same fundamentals since self-leadership is also a process of influence; however, you're influencing or leading yourself as opposed to leading others. It requires you to take control of your life and transform yourself into the person you wish to be-we may not realize it but many of us have considerable control over our lives.

Self-leadership aims to practice that type of control in a benevolent and meaningful way. The ability to lead yourself is accompanied by a vast number of benefits not only in your professional life, but also in your personal life. To name a few: Increased optimism, reduced stress, feelings of empowerment, and improved health are all manifested through the sense of control you achieve as a result of self-leadership. When done correctly, self-leadership may lead to noteworthy advancements in your career and satisfaction.

The four main principles that effective self-leadership depends on are: **purposefulness, mindfulness, reflection** and **practice**.

For now, we'll focus on purposefulness as it is the first of these principles and carries its own significance that shouldn't be overshadowed by the rest of the principles.

What Is Purposefulness?

Purposefulness refers to living in a way that indicates that you're aware of and searching for a greater meaning than mere existence. Everyone's purpose differs, some people may live with a solely financial gain as their driving force whereas others may live with the purpose to positively impact the lives of every person they encounter. Whatever it may be, purposefulness is necessary for a variety of reasons.

To start with, it offers you a clear path on which to stay so that you achieve your goals. Consider a life without purposefulness equivalent to getting in a car and having no clue of why you're there nor where you're going. The reality is that most people live their lives this way—uncertain of where they're going, drifting about with no real direction. Purpose provides you with that direction and is especially helpful when you need to make important decisions. Having purpose acts as a benchmark for you to measure alternatives against as well as provides you with the confidence you need when faced with making key decisions.

Let's say you've taken on a new role, perhaps one that requires you to go out and encourage underprivileged youth to improve their lives and make smart decisions so they would be able to break generational curses and prosper—now, if your purpose was to help people and guide them on the right path then this decision, no matter how overwhelmed you feel in the beginning stages, was the right one as it paved the way for you to achieve your purpose.

Additionally, purposefulness offers you the resilience needed to face life's inevitable uncertainties and obstacles. In the words of Vicktor Frankl, a holocaust survivor, people who have a "why" to live are able to face practically any "how".

One journey contains various paths to the same destination and this is the same when it comes to achieving your purpose—even when the time comes for you to change course and take a different path than the one you started off with; the destination remains the same and a new path shouldn't discourage you. If one way has become obsolete or doesn't provide the results you hoped for, there's always another way. The feeling that comes over you once you realize and experience this kind of control is remarkably liberating, but only possible after truly understanding your own life's purpose.

A purpose in life motivates you to chase the future instead of chasing the past—shifting your focus to where it matters: "What could be," and not "what has been." Failures and setbacks can now be regarded as temporary occurrences that assist you in your growth and improvement, as opposed to pulling you toward a permanent state of suspended animation.

Another positive effect having a purpose in life has on a person is the enhanced capacity to delay gratification since you're focusing on getting to the main destination rather than being rewarded for reaching smaller milestones. This doesn't mean milestones are not important but it simply means that you adopt the ability to put off gratification for a bit since you're oriented toward the future, so investing today for tomorrow's noteworthy rewards becomes a natural part of you.

As easy as it seems to decide what your purpose in life will be, it's actually significantly harder than one would expect. It can even be considered a lifelong pursuit that necessitates deep reflection and experience. Some people find their purpose sooner and others find it much later in life, however, the "when" is irrelevant. Embarking on the journey to find your purpose comes with its own unique benefits and by the time you've established what your purpose is, you are able to genuinely appreciate everything it took to get there.

The road to purposefulness starts with reflecting on what offers you a sense of accomplishment and happiness; from there you'll be able to see your purpose clearly and gain the confidence to pursue it.

First-Time Leader Mistakes

According to studies, approximately half of all new leaders tend to give up or fail at pursuing a path in leadership (Daskal, n.d.). New leaders have mountains of knowledge to gain, however, many don't want to accept the mistakes and challenges that come with it—probably because some mistakes may be more costly than others. Avoiding the worst of them helps build your credibility and assists you in delivering results that'll guide you toward success.

Here are some of the foundational mistakes to look out for (Daskal, n.d.):

- **Emotions getting the best of you**. Being in a position of leadership means you're required to have a certain hold on your emotions. There's no way to avoid feeling or experiencing all kinds of emotions, but letting them get the best of you implies a loss of control which is not a good quality for a leader to have. It may be appropriate to visibly express emotion in certain instances, however, generally you are expected to maintain your reserve.

- **Compromise of values.** This is often a tricky one, considering how many leaders prefer to make choices that are easier as opposed to choices that are just. You can't escape this pressure and while compromise is important in your role, remaining firm in doing the right thing will forever count in your benefit. Don't be bullied into making decisions that are unethical and against your personal values.

- **Dismissive attitude toward clear communication.** Your role as leader is to guide and provide clarity; this is what people want and expect from their leaders, so offering ambiguous instructions and poor communication will not only frustrate your subordinates, but will also increase the chances of lack of confidence in your capabilities.

- **Exhibiting domineering behavior.** Leaders who believe bullying and dominating attitudes ensures people will follow orders, is not only a terrible leader but also doesn't have a clue about what it means to be a leader. True leaders understand that the quality of people's work is directly linked to how they are treated. Encouragement is a much better motivator than fear.

- **Shifting priorities.** Inconsistency results in confusion and discord. Constantly changing your mind or shifting your opinions on what's important creates a difficult and stressful environment. It will hinder the performance of your team as well as negatively impact their opinion of you. Take the time to decide what is important and keep that as a priority.

- **Poor accessibility.** Being the leader means you're the captain of the ship—you won't find crew mates going on a hysterical hunt for the captain when important decisions have to be made. No, the captain is right there in reach and ready to steer the ship to the correct course. A leader needs to be present and available because this kind of accessibility not only keeps you in the loop of what's happening, but also makes your team more inclined to trust you. It increases morale and productivity, and if that's not enough, remember that accessibility means you're right there to provide answers and guidance without work coming to a standstill.

- **Public reprimanding.** This is actually a principle that should regularly be mentioned to all new leaders and even seasoned leaders. Reprimanding someone for a mistake they made in public, or even simply mentioning it can have dire effects. No matter what the error, address all issues in private. Stripping a person of their dignity, you will be stripped of respect.

- **Dishonesty.** It's needless to say that dishonesty diminishes trust and honesty nurtures it. Lies require a great deal of effort as you need to focus on keeping your story straight, no matter how far into the future, you need to choose your words and actions carefully to preserve your lie. Your integrity is what should be most important to you so even if you have to face the consequences of certain decisions, it's better than risking all your hard work and reputation falling apart.

These are only a few of some very common mistakes frequently made by new leaders or even experienced leaders. Others include making promises that you can't keep, having a *know-it-all* attitude, displaying favoritism, and closed-mindedness. They all show you in a negative light and you'll be faced with many avoidable challenges in your leadership. We're all human and make mistakes, just as you're not above error neither are your subordinates. Focus on setting a good tone while still upholding the values needed to achieve success.

Chapter 3

Self-Check: How to Be an Authentic Leader vs. Synthetic Leader

Getting caught up by the authoritarian title is not uncommon. While leadership is not necessarily a complicated concept, it certainly isn't simple either. This is why it's so easy to become trapped in a cycle of artificial leadership, sometimes even unknowingly. Thankfully, there are various telltale signs that help establish whether you or your leader are artificial leaders.

I've already briefly explained what artificial leadership is but let's recap it: Artificial leadership is often founded on an inflated sense of expertise and self-centeredness. Victimization by our knowledge and experience occurs when we alienate our colleagues, which in turn causes damage to the business. The only thing worse than working alongside an artificial leader is being one yourself.

The below list of signs is intended to help you evaluate your own style of leadership so you can see whether you are a manager disguised as a leader and if you relate to these, you may want to rethink your strategy to develop a more authentic leadership style.

Here are some of the telltale signs (Painter, 2014):

Lack of humility: Artificial leaders, whether they verbalize it or not, tend to believe they hold all the right answers. They seldomly apologize and even when they do, it's coordinated in a way to attract attention to themselves and aimed to offer them praise for being humble. In addition, artificial leaders may advertise their weaknesses as an attempt at authenticity.

Lack or inconsistent respect of others: A synthetic leader tends to show respect only if it's convenient to do so, or if it's part of a show or performance they're orchestrating. These leaders are also the only people in authority who frequently roll eyes during meetings, place blame on others, or offer condescending responses to people or groups. Another sign of synthetic leadership is the act of interrupting or discrediting others during meetings or presentations in order to prove a point. An authentic leader offers consistent respect to all and gives credit when credit is due. They also only correct people in private (when needed), and wait until the person presenting or speaking has concluded everything before offering feedback or insight.

Lack of partnership: The fact that they are under the illusion that they have all the answers makes partnering with others highly unacceptable to artificial leaders. The delusion is manifested when the artificial leader fails to pay respect due to others and neglects acknowledging the relative project owners and experts. This selfishness stifles the company's productivity and jeopardizes outcomes. In terms of more powerful artificial leaders, this can be regarded as a misuse of power and leads to the alienation of current and prospective working relationships. Dialogue is highly welcomed by authentic leaders, irrespective if the authentic leader considers themselves more experienced and knowledgeable—authentic leaders have no issue with conducting a dialogue about it to reach common ground. This paves the way for continuous communication and partnerships as all voices are heard and everyone feels like their opinions matter. It improves the chances of reaching an agreement too.

Lacking consistency in any of these areas simply means that you're not entirely authentic. You may be well on your way to authentic leadership; however, you just aren't there yet. Your colleagues and peers can sense inconsistency and tend to view leaders such as these as manipulative and two-faced. Consistency in humility, showing respect, and partnering with knowledgeable teammates irrespective of their role, is a quality that makes authentic leaders thrive in their field.

If you're an artificial leader you can be sure your followers are artificial too. You may think they're following you due to your perceived leadership skills when in reality they're following out of moral obligation, compliance, fear, organizational allegiance, or an amalgamation of the lot. They secretly carry a lot of resentment towards you and are likely avoiding having to engage in meaningful partnership with you. Remaining consistent in authentic leadership fosters the kind of trust from your colleagues that plays an integral part of authentic followership. Leadership of this nature produces genuine followership meaning the leader's legitimate authority becomes secondary to the followers' veritable desires to follow.

If you're not the artificial leader but find yourself having to deal with one, try using this list as a tool for improving your own development. Approach them and request feedback on your own performance as it could springboard a genuine leadership assessment. You may even spark an interest in the artificial leader to consider using this tool as well—though not getting your hopes up is also an important part of this approach as an artificial leader is not above feeling that their performance doesn't require evaluation. You may have to suck it up and be bold in order to gain some grip and don't forget that you don't have the ability to change others, only yourself.

While distinguishing artificial and authentic leadership in others may be easier, it's equally important to reflect on the positive qualities of teamwork, humility, and respect that you yourself possess. A true assessment of this is crucial to any leader's development.

Almost everyone has experienced what it's like to work with or under a synthetic leader at some point. It doesn't matter if you work in local fast-food restaurants or in Fortune 500 companies, it's impossible to escape an encounter with artificial leaders. Synthetic leadership manifests itself in a variety of forms, though, the most notable form is the delusion of a leader who considers themself much better than they actually are. People would probably jump at the chance to share their personal experiences and a conversation like that may never end, but it's important to know that the majority of leaders have experienced moments when they thought they were better than their subordinates—at some point in their career. While this isn't uncommon, what sets an artificial leader apart from an authentic leader is that the authentic leader becomes aware of this superiority complex and uses it to learn from and improve their leadership skills.

We now know how to spot a synthetic leader: They have enormous egos and inflate their expertise in the industry—this is particularly the case when it relates to employee relations and problem-solving. Another telltale sign that may have been overlooked is the attitude of knowing everything about a position they had just been promoted to. They refuse to accept guidance or help from subordinates because they feel insulted by the idea of needing help from someone in a less significant role.

It's not impossible to transform yourself from a synthetic leader to an authentic leader. Some people have the natural capabilities, while others will require some self-awareness to make it possible.

Take a look at the below principles you might want to adopt to help enhance your leadership and make it more authentic (Brown, 2021):

- **View employees as colleagues**.

    There may be a well-defined hierarchy between leader and subordinate, but there is nothing wrong with taking an approach that would be beneficial, not only to you as leader, but also your employees. That said, there's a fragile balance to ensure that you as leader are respected while at the same time not being taken advantage of by your subordinates—often the case when they consider you more of a close friend than the main authority. An authentic leader doesn't shun honest and open discussions as they invite all viewpoints and this method of engaging all employees produces more solutions and compromise as opposed to push backs and objections.

- **Practice self-awareness**.

    As you already know, this is a person's ability to recognize their own strengths and weaknesses. Understanding these two things helps a leader evaluate what it'll take to grow and learn from that knowledge. Continuously work on improving on your weaknesses, while empowering the strengths you already have.

This will bring out the best of your performance and leadership.

- **Make showing your appreciation a habit.**

    If you ever wondered what the key is to empowering your employees, appreciation is definitely it. Consistent and frequent praise of employees is something an authentic leader does willingly and happily. This isn't only telling them they've done a good job; it's also reflected in the way you treat them. Acknowledging extra efforts and hard work will make your employees want to do a great job because they'll know that what they do means a lot to you and this is a great form of motivation. It will bring out the best in them.

- **Humility, humility, humility!**

    This literally cannot be stressed enough: We're all human! No matter how knowledgeable and efficient you are at your job, no-one is above error. Mistakes are a part of life and instead of beating yourself up because you thought you knew everything, embrace the lessons that accompany your mistakes. The best authentic leaders are aware of this reality and instead of obsessing over ways to conceal their humanity (like synthetic leaders), they allow employees who may know more about a certain subject to take the wheel and present their ideas. These leaders have no issue standing back, giving credit for a good job where it is due, and openly acknowledging that they've made a mistake.

Keep in mind that at some point in our career, we all exhibit some signs of synthetic leadership. Some more than others but either way, this is what allows us to self-reflect and get back on track. Consistent practice will make learning from our experiences easier and eventually instill the values required to quickly recognize when we're slipping.

Chapter 4

Serving While You Lead

With the emergence of a new generation of leaders, *servant leadership* is slowly gaining popularity. Although, most of the time I'm met with the same question: "How do I simultaneously serve and lead?" The confusion is likely a result of our understanding of each of the individual concepts, when we hear "leader," we associate it with someone in a high rank who's surpassed mediocrity and is now showing the rest of us how to get there. The term "serve," leaves us with the understanding that the person serving is in a lower rank and possibly required to do whatever their superiors instruct them to do. This is exactly where the confusion comes in since these 2 concepts are seemingly opposing yet we're talking about servant leadership. Believe it or not, these two concepts can in fact be merged and produce spectacular results.

Leading while serving is basically the act of providing the tools and resources your team needs to be successful. It also entails allowing your workforce to develop their own efficiencies and ideas—this encourages internal development and promotion. Though this still sounds like leadership, many people are against it or frown upon this leadership method.

An example of such an occasion is when I supervised a production line at a company. The business' demands were too great for the employees to match because of the rate at which production was running. I decided to roll my sleeves up and jump in anywhere I could—loading, unloading, and more. In the midst of my efforts to help lessen the load I was pulled aside by my manager, who informed me that I was the supervisor and shouldn't be working. He literally told me that my job was to stand in front of my employees, arms crossed and push them to work faster. According to him, my very presence should motivate them to increase their productivity. Absurd right? Of course, there was no way I was going to be able to do that because my intention was to set my employees up to keep up. One of them approached me and casually mentioned that if I slowed the line down, there wouldn't be that much waste at the end of the line. He continued and said that with less waste, we'd be producing a lot more product than we were and after trying it we converted 10% of our waste to good product! (S. Brown, 2022)

Do you think that employee would've had the comfort or enthusiasm to make those suggestions had I just stood there with my arms crossed? Doubtful. By implementing the employee's suggestion, it indicated that his superior trusted him and that his input was important.

Serving while you lead has many forms—in this scenario, we saw a leader who used listening as his approach. Though the servant leader thought that providing physical assistance was what would make things easier and speed up production, it was the employee on the line who knew that an intangible resource was what was necessary to save the company tons of money. Irrespective of the fact that physical resources were not the answer, the servant leader displayed his openness to be approached, which was all it took to make a significant change to the outcome of the company's performance.

You already know that you won't have all the answers all the time so focus on establishing yourself as an approachable leader. Your team will feel comfortable to come to you with solutions that may never even have crossed your mind. Unapproachable leaders face the harsh reality of a lonely, ineffective place in this kind of leadership.

How to Serve and Lead

What does servanthood mean to you? What do you envision when you hear that word? Is it a person at the bottom of the ladder performing inferior tasks for the benefit of those higher up on the ladder? If it is, then your impression is highly flawed. Servanthood doesn't determine your position or skill. It's all about attitude.

Who can say they haven't encountered people in service roles with absolutely putrid attitudes toward servanthood? Perhaps a waiter who took their time taking your order and showed no interest in working efficiently, or the rude worker at the government agency who treated you as though your presence was an inconvenience, or even a store clerk who shamelessly chatted away on the phone with a friend rather than assist you.

As much as you can sense when a worker has no interest in helping people, you can easily sense when a worker has a servant's heart. An encounter with workers who have the attitude of servant leaders honestly changes everything, in the most spectacular ways.

We often say that the best leaders are devoted to serving others, not themselves. Ultimately the extent and quality of your influence and relationship with others depends on the sincerity and depth of your care for others.

This is precisely why it's essential for a leader to be willing to serve. Now, with that in mind, here are three habits you should actively try to form to help you to become a servant leader (Cole, 2019):

- Walk slowly through the crowd—At the next function you attend, make it your mission to connect with others by slowly circulating among them. Colleagues, clients, and employees all the same. Socialize and focus on each person you meet. If you don't already know their names, learn them! Your agenda should be establishing what each of them want, need, and desire. It may sound like a lot of unnecessary work, however, this time spent with them will help create the desire to serve them as well as build a connection with them, offering you a better understanding of how to adequately serve them.

- Implement small acts of kindness—Getting so busy that we forget about the people around us is a common thing when you're in the position of leadership. Performing small acts of kindness completely slips your mind because you have so much on your plate; however, this needs to change and starting with those closest to you should be easy. Find ways to show other people that you care about them and what they bring to the table. The positive impact such appreciation and kindness has, no matter how small, is monumental to the person on the receiving end.

- Act—No-one knows just how absent the attitude of servanthood is from your life as well as you do. If you've established that this stance is missing from your approach and views the best way to change it is to start serving. The feelings will follow the footsteps, meaning if you begin serving physically, your emotions and heart will eventually follow and reach congruence.

If success on the highest level is what you want then you need to be willing to serve on the lowest level. It's certainly the most effective way to build relationships and improve your leadership.

When asked what he thought about servant leadership, Kevin Eikenberry, a world-renowned leadership expert and two-time bestselling author, stated that he considered the word "servant" to be redundant. Before you jump to conclusions thinking that the next section will contradict everything we've spoken about up until this point, understand that he does indeed believe in the concept of servant leadership and views the lessons from what you learn and read about it as extremely valuable. However, the reason for the opinion that the "servant" part of it is redundant is because service is an underlying component of leadership.

By definition, a leader is someone trying to move toward a specific desired future and hopefully a future that those you are leading see as desirable too. This includes communities and customers. Being a leader involves taking action to do what is needed to achieve that desired future and this in itself, is an act of service. Utilizing your knowledge, skills, insights and intellect to manufacture something greater than yourself.

Below are some suggestions on how to effectively serve while leading and take the time to consider how often you already incorporate these into your leadership style, also how often you could implement them. Appreciate that these aren't mere schemes to simply reach your destination, they are tools to produce the best you can as well as the bring the best out of others. Applying these methods with any intention other than to be of service will significantly hinder your results and leave you disappointed and possibly with a damaged reputation.

Listen. This seems to have made another appearance on the list and can you guess why? Because of how many people feel they're not being listened to in nearly every aspect of their lives, not only in the workplace. Listening to people means you are serving a key internal need, solidifying trust, building a better relationship, learning new information, ideas, and perspectives that can help steer you toward the goals we're all trying to achieve.

Respond. The reason why people want us to listen is because they want to be heard. Leaders are frequently asked questions about procedures and processes, ideas and challenges, resources and various other things and the only way to make others feel heard is by responding. Our answers are oftentimes not the ones they were hoping for but from a perspective of serving those we lead we are required to respond to their queries and requests.

Engage. This is essentially the combination or result of listening and responding, however, there is much more to it than simple mathematics. It's not about the important but popular idea of engaging with others— it's about taking a look in the mirror and ascertaining if you truly are engaging with those you lead. Do you have conversations with them, share with them, and generally engage with them with matters beyond the standard discourse of work?

Ask. If you genuinely want to know how people are feeling, what ideas they have, or how they can influence greater results, then you need to ask them. When last have you had a discussion with your workforce asking them how things are holding up with them, what concerns they have, or if they have any new ideas they want to share? It's time to go back to your team and ask them a bunch of questions so they know that you don't only care about productivity and the success of the business, but about them as the ones responsible for your productivity and success too.

Care. If someone is serving others surely you can tell that there's a sense of care driving those actions and behaviors, right? Caring for those you lead is another form of serving them. Caring about their aspirations, values, and concerns doesn't mean that you're everyone's best friend, but it does mean that you have genuine person to person compassion and concern for them. When done from the heart, these acts of caring may lead to better results than any process map or scoping document could ever produce.

Though these suggestions may have many going "No, that's far too sensitive and emotional for a leader," it really isn't. Including this as an authentic part of your leadership approach will make an enormous difference in the lives of those following you as well as the overall performance and results you achieve.

The realization that leadership is an act of service will better equip you for success. Though you need to remember that not everything you implement as leader will be agreed with or welcomed; still, keep the service of others in pursuit of admirable goals as your main focus as it'll help you lead with great compassion and in return, offer great results.

Challenges of Servant Leadership

As with everything in life, challenges are inescapable and considering how crucial choosing an effective leadership model is to the operation and success of a business, one must try to prepare for almost any challenge. The servant leadership style has increased in popularity in recent years because the needs of employees and motivating them to perform at their best, is the focal point of this strategy.

This model was first developed in 1970 by Robert K. Greenleaf. It dismisses traditional authoritarian attitudes most businesses favor and replaces it with business owners who are responsive and empathetic to the needs of employees in the professional as well as personal aspects of their growth. In terms of management, servant leadership encourages the delegation of tasks while still providing continuous support to the team by means of research, gathering supplies and resources, and continuing education (Kokemuller, n.d.).

This model of leadership may be effective, however, it's imperative that you understand some of the limitations it may have before deciding if this is the most effective strategy for your company.

Could lead to less motivated employees

Because of the servant leaders' nature to step in and resolve problems when they occur, excessive "rescuing" may cause employees to be less motivated to work hard. This will certainly affect the results they produce over time as they become comfortable with the fact that their leader will step in and handle whatever needs attention. It often leaves them more tempted to slack off and exert less effort in their duties.

Sacrificing traditional authority

This may very well be one of the most obvious limitations of servant leadership since it requires leaders to surrender their absolute authority. It opposes traditional workplace structures such as the CEO makes all business decisions, communicates the decisions to the subordinates, and receives the credit when those decisions are implemented by workers. As the servant leader, one of the challenges you may face is the repression of your ego. This model's main focus is the employees and helping them exceed performance standards. Selflessness is a tough trait to come by in the corporate world, especially since most business owners believe surrendering their authority would negatively impact their success.

Not suited for every business

This is exactly what it sounds like. Unfortunately, not every business can benefit from this approach because establishing successful servant leadership methods takes time as it necessitates steadfastness in your commitment to developing your staff and the encouragement of personal and professional growth. Typically, businesses undergoing changes in its work culture may not respond positively to servant leadership. The lack of stability makes it harder for managers to implement this system and is especially true when good-hearted managers prioritize the feelings of employees, as opposed to their needs. Caring too much about offending or hurting an employee's feelings leads to reluctance in making difficult decisions or dishonest performance critiques.

Decreases managerial authority

It should be needless to say that placing the needs of your employees at the very top of your priorities can result in the minimization of the authority of the general management function in your business. Employees who witness their superiors catering to their needs with utmost importance may become less likely to view those superiors as authoritarian figures. Additionally, if an occasion arises where the servant leader is expected to resume their more dominant role for the purpose of pushing employees to achieve better in their performance, they mind the transition extremely difficult and sometimes even impossible. Empathy cannot simply be imitated but understanding the distinction between boss and employee is very necessary, so one can see why servant leadership could make this quite the task.

A business owner is therefore recommended to take a hard look at their organizational structure to decide if servant leadership is the approach they want to go with, regardless of these disadvantages.

How to Be a Servant Leader Without the Burnout

So many leaders are finding themselves exhausted and battling to stay afloat. They're not using their vacation time and working much longer hours with minimal prospects for change. Servant leadership can seriously take a toll on you as the leader since you want to be available at all times to guide and support your team.

Servant leadership has numerous benefits, some of which are (Janzen, 2021):

-   It creates a positive working environment.
-   Manifests a culture of belonging.
-   Builds commitment, loyalty and trust.
-   Fosters improved collaboration and stronger team unity.
-   Promotes better innovation and new ideas.

Even with all these wonderful attributes servant leadership has to offer, it can be taken too far and cause dire consequences as a result. Embracing this method with little to no boundaries often places leaders at risk.

Research has revealed that employees and leaders are both impending burnouts. As a matter of fact, 60% of leaders claim they feel depleted by the end of the day, which is a clear sign of burnout(Janzen, 2021).

Mayo Clinic provided some additional indicators which are (Janzen, 2021):

-   A lack of energy needed to be productive
-   Developing cynicism or becoming overly critical of others
-   Difficulty concentrating
-   Irritability or impatience with clients or coworkers

- Lack of satisfaction in the workplace
- Indigestion, headaches, or sleeping problems

In relation to servant leadership, the cycle usually looks like this: Employees become burned out, so the leaders step in to assist and support the employees, causing them to burn out in the process. This cycle is not only dangerous for everyone, it also creates a dilemma for leaders. Insisting on stepping in every time their team needs them puts them at risk of burning themselves out; however, if they choose not to step in and help, things could escalate and worsen for the employees. So, what's to be done now? Should the leader go back to the traditional leadership approach of control and command or risk not leveraging talent?

Not at all. There is actually a better way.

Have you ever heard the pre-flight speech on a plane? The one where you're told to put your oxygen mask on first before you attempt to assist others. Children are usually used as an example in this case. It may seem counterintuitive but it makes sense. Let's say your children survive but you don't, who will be there to take care of them when you're gone? A leader needs to view their employees and job from this perspective: If you don't take care of yourself first, the people who depend on you will have no guidance and become lost. Figure out what in your role and job, is the equivalent to the oxygen mask on the plane. Which support systems are needed to serve others and prevent you from feeling consumed at the end of the day.

Once again, there is no one-size fits all approach in this matter. There are however a few steps you can take to figure out what works best for you.

Establish complete clarity on your big picture. Envision your company's future as well as your future role. Take some time out to get clarity on what your big picture is, as it'll help you find joy and fulfillment in your daily tasks. Starting your day with your big picture in mind will help you remain focused on what's important and what isn't. That's how you decide which tasks are worth spending extra energy on and which aren't.

Ascertain out what motivates your team. Give your employees projects that inspire and encourage them, it will help reduce symptoms of burnout. In order to effectively incorporate this you will have to identify internal motivation and regulate and delegate projects accordingly.

Set boundaries. Your instinct may be to draw a hard, visible line that shall not be passed; however, we've already learned that this method is ineffective. Rather get clarity on what is essential and what isn't. Take all of the projects on your plate and your team's plate into consideration and determine what is crucial and what aligns with your big picture.

The above may help you reduce your own burnout and that of your team and remember that if you're feeling burned out, ignore the voices in your head telling you to keep pushing and grinding with your head down. This is not healthy and will eventually come back to bite you. There's no shame in taking a step back and putting your oxygen mask on first. It'll lead to a healthier, more capable you, and result in better support for your team.

Chapter 5

Being an Aspirin, in Spite of Your Migraine

Life is unpredictable—it has its good days and its bad days, and not just for you as a leader but for your employees as well. The headache of paying bills, getting the kids ready for school, or relationship problems can become quite intense and too much for anyone to handle.

Which leaves us asking: How can you as leader lead your team to perform its best in spite of their own headaches. Additionally, how can you be the aspirin to your team's headache when you've got headaches of your own? Leaders can actually consider themselves as a first aid cabinet. With various symptoms all around the workplace, your role is to establish what kind of aid is necessary to fix each individual problem.

Below are some ways you can practice being a proverbial aspirin irrespective of your own headache (S. Brown, 2022b):

Set aside time to practice mindfulness—Mindfulness emphasizes the importance of focusing on the present. Basically, it means that you focus less on events of the past or future because the past can't be changed and the future is extremely unpredictable. Remaining focused on the present and which actions you can take to make the most of it now, is what is referred to as a mindful spirit. Mindfulness means that as opposed to punishing yourself for mistakes you've made in the past or obsessing over possible future challenges, you prioritize dealing with the tasks at hand. Stepping out of your office or finding a quiet place to just close your eyes and listen to the minutest sounds and details around you can be very helpful to stay focused on the present.

Genuinely listen when employees are sharing their problems— A person who walks into the office with treats for the whole team and a broad smile every day, isn't exempt from experiencing bad days. We're all only human and we all face challenges in life. The manner in which to deal with this is to be available when your employees need to get a load off their chest. In most instances, all they need is a listening ear and this could be a perfect opportunity for you, as leader, to practice your active listening skills. Additionally, you may even find yourself sharing some of your own challenges with that employee and in doing so, indicate to them that you're just as vulnerable as they are and can relate to them. This session may also help you manage your own headache and offer comfort you may not have realized you needed.

Allow everyone to take-5—More and more studies are revealing that a work-life balance approach is more effective than the typical work-dominant approach that so many workers are battling with. Much like a yawn, if one employee is having a bad day, the entire office seems to be affected by it. If you notice this attitude and behavior among your team, give them a short break to regroup and unwind even if it is just for 5 minutes. That little time out of that negative energy can do wonders. If there are smaller teams whose temporary joint absence won't affect productivity too much, they can be sent out for lunch together. In the case of larger teams, give everyone an additional 10-15 minutes on their break—even if you have to order ice-cream bars, anything positive and different will help lighten everyone's load.

Escaping the challenges of life unfortunately is not an option so remember that you're not the only one facing those challenges-everyone is. Practicing mindfulness will help lighten your mental load. Make it clear to your team that you're truly interested in hearing what they have to say. Also, don't be afraid to give everyone some time to just chill and gather themselves so that they can come back fresh.

Managing an Employee Facing a Personal Crisis

From time to time, we're all faced with life events that distract us from work, whether it's the death of someone close to us, marital problems, or sickness of a family member. No matter what it is, as a leader, you can't expect the best performance from an employee going through something like this. You should ask yourself how you can emotionally support that employee while ensuring that they're doing their work (or as much of it as they can do).

According to Harvard Business School professor and author of *Being the Boss*, Linda Hill, one of the true challenges all bosses face is managing an employee who is facing a stressful or difficult period. For the most part, we try our utmost to keep home and work separate, however, there are some situations where we have no control of the collision of our personal and professional lives. How you as the leader handle these situations with employees often tests the quality of your leadership. While you're required to be compassionate and empathetic, you're also required to be professional and keep the productivity of your team in mind. This fine line to maintain can overwhelm many leaders but here are some ways on how to manage this effectively.

- **Availability:** A leader's first challenge is often recognizing the warning signs of an employee who is facing a difficult time. Employees generally don't feel comfortable coming to their leader to discuss family or relationship problems and may even be embarrassed that these are the reasons behind their habitual lateness or failure to be productive. This is why it's important to invest time in building good relationships with employees so that you'll be able to notice early on if something is off with them, or they may be comfortable coming to you to let you know. An atmosphere of compassion in the office makes people more likely to proactive come to you with any personal issues they know may be affecting their work. They would respect you enough to want to let you know why their performance has been subpar and will be open to hearing some of your recommendations to resolve it.

- **Don't pry:** Your role as leader in situations like these is to show care and empathy, this in no way suggests that you should assume the role of an employee's personal confidante. After all, your job is managing and leading the team for the success of the business, not to be everyone's therapist. This means avoiding asking too many questions about the employee's problem. Since you're the one with the most authority in the encounter, the employee may feel obligated to share information they're not comfortable sharing. Your aim is to develop a caring relationship with that employee, not a friendly relationship. A common mistake many leaders make is that they confuse being trusted and respected with being liked. You can accomplish the same compassionate support of an employee through trust and respect without them liking you. As the leader of the team your concern isn't only understanding the needs and concerns of your team, it's doing so while still keeping everyone focused on accomplishing work. Being overly involved in your employee's problems could lead to them assuming that you'd understand if work took a major back seat until they're emotionally stable again. This is unhelpful to the employee as well as to you and the business. Employees should know that you empathize with their situation and don't mind giving them some time to get themselves in order but this time cannot be unnecessarily prolonged nor can it be a regular occurrence. You will lose the respect of other employees as they may think you are displaying favoritism or that they too, can take advantage of this.

- **First listen, then suggest:** When an employee is addressing you about their current struggles, try to avoid immediately advocating for some specific course of action. You don't necessarily know if that's what they wanted, yet you've jumped the gun and put it out there. Perhaps all they want is a sounding board regarding the struggles of caring for a sick relative or they may simply want to explain to you why they've been so absentminded in their work lately. Immediately suggesting a leave of absence may offend them, if that wasn't what they wanted. Rather try asking the employee how you can address the issue together. Using the word "we" also helps in making it sound less like you're placing the blame on the employee and more like you're willing to do your part in helping them achieve optimal performance again. For example, "How can *we* support you during this tough time?" The employee may already have an idea for a temporary arrangement that is reasonable and agreeable to you, such as handing a project over to a colleague, some time off, or a more flexible temporary schedule.

- **Know what you can offer:** Though you may be perfectly happy offering a grieving employee time off for a few weeks or allowing a woman with a high-risk pregnancy the ability to work from home; however, the final decision may not always lie with you. If you work for a business that offers you the freedom to exercise flexible schedules at your own discretion, then great, do what you think is best. If your company typically has a lot of restrictions on short or long-term leave, first check your capacity and what you can offer that employee before making any commitments. Explain to them that you need to confirm what options are available in situations like that.

- **Check in on them:** You should do this even if you haven't yet settled on a solution. Occasionally either drop by the desk to see if they're still doing okay, or send a brief email just checking in— remember to still be mindful of their privacy. Your employee will not only appreciate your efforts and concern, but you'll be able to be updated on how they're coping and may find that your employee no longer needs what you requested initially. They may need less time off, or simply limited tasks for a few weeks. Don't imply that the employee looks better or anything, you can simply ask, "Do you think you have a better handle on it?" And their response should then trigger what steps should be taken next. Remember to ask them to keep in touch so that you both know where you stand and are not met with surprises at the end of the day. Furthermore, let them know that your door is still open even though they feel better and that you're always willing to do some more problem solving where necessary.

- **Consider workload:** Unfortunately, compassion isn't the only thing you have to worry about. You also have to establish the effects that prolonged absence will have on clients and team members. If there are in fact some risks to consider, you may need to reduce those risks by easing that person's workload. If you've already delegated some of that employee's tasks to other team members, feel free to take on some of those tasks yourself. Also remember to reward the people who are stepping in to help lighten that load. You should also set timelines for whatever adjustments you've made so that you can meet with that employee before the end of the timeline to establish what the situation is at that point and ways forward. No matter the adjustment you make, be sure that your expectations during that period are clear and realistic.

- **Be consistent and transparent:** You need to understand that other employees will be paying attention to how you treat the struggling employee and will likely expect similar treatment should they experience difficulty in the future. Leaders who get their teams to work productively are those who've shown their team that they can be trusted in moments of treating everyone fairly. As unique as each situation is, you may want to be acquainted with policies in the event that you may need to apply them more than once. Some solutions can apply to the next person and the one after that and so one.

Important Principles to keep in mind (O'Hara, 2018):

- Do's:
    - Think of creative solutions. Flexible schedules allow the person to continue their work without disrupting their productivity too much.
    - Set the tone of compassion in the workplace. This not only gives your employees confidence to come to you with their

struggles, but also gives you the chance to detect warning signs.

- Check in regularly. This is not only to ensure that the employee is okay and coping, it's also to reassure them that they still have your support and to establish if there are any additional accommodations to be made.

- Don'ts:
  - Behave like a therapist. You're the leader of the group and though your heart may be in the right place, unfortunately you cannot allow yourself to get involved in your employee's personal affairs.
  - Make commitments you can't fulfill. Ensure that you possess the knowledge of your company's policies before making any adjustments or decisions regarding work arrangements.
  - Address similar situations among employees differently. Remember that your employees are watching and taking notes of what you're willing to do for the one. Being unwilling to offer them the same solution or being inconsistent will result in resentment and oftentimes discord.

This kind of responsibility can surely take a toll on your own health and mental state so take time out to yourself to clear your head and unwind. You may need to go for a walk among nature, a bike ride in the park, or even just a 15 minutes chill outside to take in the fresh air and relax a bit. Don't allow yourself to become overwhelmed or burned out—soon as you feel like you're not in the right headspace to be making adequate decisions, speak to the employee and explain to them that you're just a bit stressed and will sit with them as soon as you've gotten yourself sorted. Remember to let them know that the time away is not because you don't want to deal with them and their concerns, you just want to ensure that you're in the correct frame of mind to fully understand their situation, so you can make effective decisions that'll be suited for both them as well as the business.

Chapter 6

Servant Leadership

While some may only be hearing about this term now, servant leadership isn't a new concept. The implementation of servant leaders within corporations is done to improve the performance of the company as a whole. We've already learned various fundamentals surrounding servant leadership, however in this section, we explore it a little more in detail.

Let's have a look at some of the benefits of being a servant leader. Traditional leaders are all over, and most of us have experienced being under their leadership—they probably make up the majority of leaders in the world of business. However, with the emergence of a new generation of business, we are witnessing a strong positive change toward servant leadership with the mental health and work-life balance becoming the focal point for employers.

Traditional leadership focuses on improving the business too, although this is generally accomplished by leadership making all the decisions and everyone else having to simply fall in line. Additionally, traditional leadership places a company at risk of losing buy-in from employees at entry-level which results in the loss of efficiency, motivation, morale, and loyalty of existing employees. Oftentimes, traditional leadership also lacks respect for employees whereas servant leadership is centered around placing the needs of the employee first. Servant leaders focus on praising, developing, and eventually promoting employees from within.

A leader who develops their employees shows appreciation for that employee and contrary to traditional leadership, this fosters efficiency, accountability, motivation and morale. Being part of a respected team makes us want to see our team perform well.

Let's have a recap on the characteristics of a servant leader (Brown, 2021):

Empathy

This is an essential and great characteristic of servant leadership. Though, I prefer to call it "connecting". Connection is about considering a situation from multiple perspectives. The workplace is filled with people with different opinions and different viewpoints. Empathy or connecting with them is what allows you to put yourself in their shoes and see how certain decisions impact each employee. This is a sign of respect and will expand your knowledge.

Listening Skills

The listening skills referred to here is active listening, and is necessary for all leaders. Listening skills are a way of showing your employees that their opinions matter to you, acknowledging their expertise and instilling trust that they can come to you when they need help. Though listening to understand can be challenging, developing this skill will take you places.

Encouragement

Our days have become so monotonous and few people feel fully satisfied with this so offering your employees praise is one way to keep people motivated—it can, however, only go so far. Encouraging them means helping employees elevate their ambitions. Servant leaders know exactly how to nurture and develop an employee so that the employee can enhance their skills and expertise, hopefully moving on to improved career choices within the company.

Selflessness

This means helping others succeed without prioritizing your intent to fast-track up the company ladder. It also means not taking credit for the hard work of the employees or minimizing their efforts. As a servant leader you're required to develop and give praise where it's due so that everyone within the company has the opportunity to prosper.

If you want to become a servant leader you need to focus on cultivating trust and developing your employees. To accomplish this, you'll need to improve your empathy and listening skills as well as give praise where praise is due as to improve the individuals in your team and the company's overall growth.

The Origins of Servant Leadership

Most people have heard of the term "servant leadership," because of how often it gets used in business conversations nowadays, especially when referencing scrum masters or agile coaches. It completely contrasts leadership styles adopted from Kantian theory which gives the leader utmost authority over their subordinates.

If you've ever wondered what this term means and why it seems a bit paradoxical then you're in luck. In this section we'll cover the origins of this form of leadership as well as look at some famous servant leaders we can look to for inspiration.

In the 5th century B.C, a Chinese philosopher described the concept of servant leadership. He postulated that a preeminent rule is one who deflects attention, saying: "The sage is self-effacing and scanty of words. When his task is accomplished and things have been completed, all the people say, 'We ourselves have achieved it.'"(Patel, n.d.)

Ancient scriptures also contain further examples of servant leadership. The values of virtue of Buddhism very closely align with the teachings of servant leadership. For instance, instead of promoting how we should behave, servant leadership emphasizes what kind of people we should be. There are numerous similarities between the values of servant leadership and the biblical worldview that asserts that kindness towards others leads to compassion toward others.

Though the concept was present since this time, it wasn't until the 1970s that servant leadership became associated with leadership roles in business.

In 1970, a management expert named Robert K. Greenleaf explained how he conceptualized the idea after reading German writer Hermann Hesse's *Journey to the East*. The novel tells of a group of knowledge seekers in search of the ultimate truth. One of the group members was a servant named Leo, who had a positive attitude and sang songs which kept their spirits high. He also performed menial chores for the group. One day, Leo disappeared and this caused the group to fall into chaos. Their journey had come to an abrupt end. One of the individuals of the group ran into Leo a few years later and learned that Leo was actually the official head of the Order that had sponsored their expedition, yet he had been their servant and nobly led their group (Patel, n.d.).

Considering that Leo's leadership was bestowed upon him by others, it could have been revoked just as easily, but due to his servant heart and nature it couldn't have been taken away. In his publication, *The Servant as Leader*, Greenleaf stated that this particular story clearly shows how a great leader is seen as a servant first, which is the key to his greatness. He goes on to say that servant leaders are not driven by the traditional presentations of power. It starts with the inherent desire to want to serve and through conscious choice, one aspires to lead. This kind of person is distinctly different to those who are leaders first, possibly because of the need to satisfy an unusual sense of power or material gains (Patel, n.d.).

The differences manifest themselves in how the leader handles other people's needs.

Greenleaf's assertion is therefore that servant leaders are not motivated by power, not the urge for individual success.

Why Is Servant Leadership Becoming So Important?

If the global pandemic has taught us anything it would be that during a time of unprecedented challenge, service should be placed above self. Everyone has been affected by the pandemic not only individually but also as organizations and as a society. We battled to find new ways to work and function effectively as new unknown challenges crept up on us. Challenges such as laying off some of our staff, loss of income, finding new ways to operate from all over the world, and ways to keep staff who had no choice but to work from company offices safe from sickness. Broader societal impacts included damaging effects of the global economy. This is what calls for a more comprehensive and communal leadership style—a leadership approach that focuses on serving others.

Even though one would like to believe that those in vital fields such as global development or health care automatically possess the values of caring and serving others, this simply is not the case as not every leader represents these qualities. Money and power can cause leaders to lose sight of their unselfish goals, even in caring professions. This means they're likely leading organizations without prioritizing service to society and the community.

The differences between servant leaders and leaders who prioritize their own egocentric goals are(Neale, 2020):

- Servant leaders focus mainly on the growth and well-being of others and their community.
- Servant leaders are fine sharing power if it will lead to the overall success of everyone.
- Servant leaders place other people's needs ahead of their own and empower their team through development and growth, and encourage them to perform at their best.

Greenleaf also mentions how servant leadership used to be the foundation of a good society, since caring was an individual responsibility. In today's age, caring is delivered through corporations and institutions that are oftentimes very impersonal, large, complex, sometimes inadequate and often corrupt. Collectively, however, corporations have the capacity to change the world by creating just, improved and more compassionate societies through increased opportunities. This is only accomplishable if we increase our organization's capacity and willingness to serve. Before all this though, their operations and those operating them need to be examined. The capacity to change societies can only be developed by developing people in which case servant leadership should be allowed the necessary conditions to prosper and thrive.

To instill the qualities of servant leadership in ourselves we need to actively practice the characteristics of a servant leader previously mentioned. One by one we'll be able to change the attitudes and mindsets of most people and in turn create a society where the service of others will remain the focal point.

Four Famously Exceptional Servant Leaders

There may be many well-known and some unknown worthy servant leaders out there, however, these 5 people left legacies that teach volumes about leadership success and effectiveness. They each share similar praiseworthy qualities while still highlighting a key trait that sets them apart. They all prioritized giving as opposed to taking and this quality by itself, places their honor above everything else.

Mother Teresa

Born in Albania, Mother Teresa became a Roman Catholic nun, who served in Ireland and later moved to India. India's perpetual poverty didn't sit well with her, so she diligently served poor and dying people by living among them and providing each one with comfort. People from all over the world couldn't help but be touched by her unrelenting compassion. Much like all great servant leaders, she valued and loved people—later founding Missionaries of Charity. With so much support and awe from people all over, the charity eventually grew to 4500 sisters in 133 countries. Her principal devotion was to the poor or the dying. She gained worldwide admiration and respect. Her statement, "I have found the paradox–that if you love until it hurts, there can be no more hurt, only more love," is proof that she lived by the values of servant leadership.

Mahatma Gandhi

Born and raised in the Hindu merchant caste system, Mr. Gandhi was quite an ordinary boy but he was filled with the determination to do well. He received law training in London; however, during his time as an expatriate lawyer practicing civil disobedience in South Africa, he experienced the harshness of racism. He then returned to India and became an activist, organizing peasants, laborers, and farmers to gain social justice. He further achieved leadership in the Indian National Congress which resulted in national campaigns for self-rule and was arrested by the government on thirteen different occasions. When he spoke about his struggles, he stated that strength is not derived from a physical capacity but rather from an unyielding will—appealing for non-cooperation through his book, Hind Swaraj. Mr. Gandhi's non-violent approach bewildered British rule. He believed that you can shake the world in a gentle way. As a result of his non-aggressive approach, he captured the attention of people worldwide which incited rallies for freedom and global movements. This is what led to India's eventual independence. Many of us know the famous quote where he instructs us to be the change we wish to see in the world. Even though pointing it out may not be necessary, I'm going to do it anyway, here we can see that his actions were never about him personally, instead they were about the Indian people and justice.

Abraham Lincoln

He grew up in the western frontier and didn't have much. In fact, he was quite poor and was mostly self-educated. He was a store clerk and on one occasion he realized that he had shortchanged a customer by a few pennies, he walked miles to rectify this mistake—this action gave him the title of "honest Abe." This need to rectify his mistakes was not a one-time occurrence as it happened several times and people grew to openly admire and praise his integrity. This led to him being requested to judge disputes, which eventually led him to practice law. While this quality is admirable, his most enduring one was his perseverance. His various personal difficulties are what prepared him for his future role. He even stated at one time that one cannot fail unless one quits. You may be surprised to learn that he not only had two failed businesses but also lost 8 political elections. He additionally suffered a nervous breakdown and became bedridden for 6 months. Even with all this, he became the 16th President of the United States and served his nation through some of its most trying times during the Civil War. He helped to preserve the nation and was responsible for the abolishment of slavery. The federal government was also strengthened through his help which positioned the US for world impact many years later. To this day, Lincoln is regarded as one of the USA's finest presidents.

Nelson Mandela

Mandela's activism and view on equality is what led to his 27-year imprisonment. He was abused and suffered inhumane treatment and torture. Despite all of this, he earned his bachelor's degree while serving his prison sentence. If this isn't impressive enough, Mandela also smuggled a draft of his book, Long Walk to Freedom, out of prison. When he was finally released from prison, he negotiated with F.W de Klerk, to end apartheid. This was successfully accomplished during a time of political instability and extreme racial tension. The two consequently won the Nobel Peace prize as a result of their efforts. Mandela later became the first black president of South Africa. This selfless and determined way of leadership is what paved the way for this enormous change to the country. Like many other servant leaders, he possessed the extraordinary quality of forgiveness and created a multi-racial government. Mandela's outstanding devotion to unity and peace gave him a global audience and stage.

This is the section of the chapter where we sit back and appreciate that the success of these leaders wasn't money, power, or personal gain. The secret to their success is the path of servant leadership which, no matter what obstacles they faced, they did not deviate from. Their cause was more important to them than their own lives. If today's leaders would only learn from these examples and consider them as role models because leadership greatness has nothing to do with gaining and everything to do with giving.

Chapter 7

Leading Not Lording

If you're currently a leader or have the professional aspiration to become a leader one day, you without a doubt have an ocean of online articles and books at your disposal for guidance. I would, however, like you to take a step back and ask yourself what kind of leader you'd want to have. If you're having trouble understanding why that's relevant or if you're having trouble reaching an answer, consider these questions: Do you want a leader whose approach is intimidation of micromanagement? Or do you want a leader who empowers you?

I'm almost positive you'd want a leader who empowers you and brings out the best of your abilities. The beauty of empowerment is that it fosters trust and improves morale in a business. You'll come across numerous insights leading you to believe that being a good leader is an unfathomable challenge yet the reality or rather the first step to being a great leader is looking within yourself.

Eliminating Micromanagement Builds Trust

To lead without lording over your employees requires you to build trust in them and it begins with taking a step back. The opposite of this action is what we call micromanagement and many of us have heard this term before.

The micromanagement leadership style casts trust aside and typically creates a work environment of aggressiveness, low performance, and a high-turnover. Persistent scrutiny leads to ineffectiveness in employees, they tend to lose creativity or feel as though there is no place for their ideas and feedback. Workers working under conditions of micromanagement cause employees to eventually expect their jobs to be fully laid out for them and generally develop low morale-which in turn results in an increase in mistakes. These effects have a ripple effect and ultimately leaves the leader with more work.

Some of the usual actions of a micromanager include:

- involving themselves in other people's work
- reluctance to delegate tasks
- obsessing over finer details so unable to see the bigger picture
- dishearten others from making decisions on their own if the decision wasn't run by them
- disloyal to colleagues
- teams lack motivation
- improper priorities
- disregard colleague expertise and experience
- focus on least important or irrelevant information

Lead With Trust

The strongest leaders are those who build teams that prosper under empowerment as opposed to control. The fact that employees are employed based on their ability to do a job should be praised and acknowledged rather than disregarded or ignored. This is precisely why an effective leader avoids controlling the employee—instead they consider leadership as a resource for employees to utilize for their own benefit and the company alike.

Becoming a resource means providing tools that allow empowered employees to excel and succeed; an employee's success results in the leader's success.

Consider the below ways to become a positive resource for your employees:

- **Have clear objectives**—A leader who provides clear objectives sets expectations for every employee. Doing so eliminates room for the nature of ambiguity that is common in various micromanaged offices. Each employee understands what their role is and are tools needed to satisfactorily achieve their goals.
- **Being open to feedback**—Providing feedback as well as being open to it is one of the most important factors that stand out to employees in a comfortable work environment. The act of being open to feedback and suggestions produces an open atmosphere in the workplace. Many employees consider being heard as a powerful tool of recognition.
- **Offer honest and consistent communication**—Having strong communication with your team institutes knowledge and trust between a leader and their employees. Communication doesn't only involve giving instruction where needed, it also includes

having one-on-one discussions about performance, goals, and expectations. They may also include listing resources available to the employee and most importantly: displaying a willingness to take the employee's suggestions and feedback.

When you avoid lording over your employees and lead them instead, you empower them to do what they'd been hired to do. You can establish a powerful workforce if you create strong communication, offer clear direction and resources, and encourage feedback.

Effects of Micromanagement

Nothing demotivates employees like having a micromanaging boss controlling or scrutinizing their every move. Trinity solutions conducted a survey which showed that (Petrova, 2021):

- 79% of the participants had experienced being micromanaged
- 69% admitted to wanting to change jobs as a result of micromanagement
- 36% actually went through with changing jobs
- 71% attributed micromanagement to an interference with their performance
- 85% admitted to their moral being negatively affected

In the next section of this chapter, we'll discuss micromanagement in greater detail. What it is, why people feel the need to micromanage, what signs to look out for, how to handle or cope with a boss that is micromanaging you, and how to prevent yourself from continuing the micromanaging cycle.

What Is Micromanaging?

Micromanagement is a term used to describe a particular management style, usually with negative undertones. This kind of management style consists of excessive supervision and attempts to control employees and their work processes. It also entails limiting an employee's decision-making, exhibiting reluctance to delegating work, and possessing an unhealthy obsession with information-gathering.

Why Do People Choose a Micromanagement Approach?

Because the decision to micromanage is subjective to whomever has chosen this approach, the answer to this question is just as subjective. This decision can be due to a variety of reasons such as an extreme need for control, inexperience, fear of failure, unqualified team members, insecurities, or simply an unhealthy ego. The list goes on; however, it's not uncommon for some micromanagers to have decided on this approach as a result of instability or issues in their personal lives. That said, the most common reasons for micromanagement is due to a lack of trust in the abilities of colleagues or team members, or a general lack of respect for them.

Signs of a Micromanager

If you've ever wonder whether you're being micromanaged or even if you yourself are micromanaging your team, have a look at the telltale signs of micromanagement:

Avoiding delegation

They usually have the idea that no-one is capable of doing a good job other than them, so they intentionally avoid delegating work to other workers and do everything themselves. Needless to say, this method hardly works out well for anyone since they're not superheroes or capable of doing absolutely everything alone. They need to come back down to Earth and understand that the tasks should be handed over to the people with the specialized skills and qualifications needed to produce desirable results.

Involving themselves in employees' work

Almost everyone understands how frustrating and annoying it can be to have someone constantly standing over your shoulder watching every move you make and persistently checking in on what you do—not only that, it's highly ineffective. Many people become extremely uncomfortable with being watched all the time which could lead to unnecessary stress on that individual as well as additional errors. Some people handle it so badly that they freeze entirely.

Constantly wanting updates and status reports

We can understand weekly check-ins and status reports since it is probably a part of standard procedure; however, when employees are being asked for daily updates, this is a sure sign of either being micromanaged or micromanaging your team. This is a horrid obsession which wastes time, time that could've been spent doing their actual job but instead they're being requested to create unnecessary detailed reports half the time.

Expecting to be cc'd into every email

This is typically requested because either you as leader or your manager (if you're an employee), wants visibility on every bit of communication at all times because of the fear of being left out of the loop. It could also be as a result of a fear that discussions or decisions are being made behind their back.

Constantly complain and are never satisfied

They tend to complain about everything even when there's no reason for it at all. The reality is that a constant search for flaws and mistakes in others leads to that being the only thing you find. These complaints often have nothing to do with the actual execution of the tasks and are so small that they could simply have been let go. Common misperception micromanagers have about this approach is that they are encouraging perfection yet all they're doing is draining employees of their motivation.

Discouraging independent decision-making and diminishing initiative and creativity

How do they diminish creativity and initiative? Well, I'm glad you asked! Their lack of trust in the capabilities of others to efficiently do their jobs, they simply tell employees what to do. This downright extinguishes any creative ideas or initiatives they may have already had. Constantly being told exactly how to do something you've been employed to do because you know how to do it, can be maddening and discouraging.

The freedom of independent decision-making is another unthinkable act to micromanagers. Yes, your work likely has to undergo some kind of approval from a senior, but this should mean that you have absolutely no decisions in the process of your own work. You were hired because of your expertise in your field and your own creative input may even lead the company to more growth and returns.

Failing to pass on knowledge and skills

To many, leaders and managers are their role models, especially to those just starting out. They're hungry for guidance but if the manager has no interest in teaching their subordinates, it's not only disappointing but also daunting and discouraging. In addition to not getting the guidance they hope for, employees are faced with continuous complaints which could make them either make them give up or turn them into dreadful micromanagers in future.

How to Handle a Micromanaging Boss

No-one enjoys being micromanaged. The constant stress of doing everything the way your manager wants, being shouted at, or waking up in the mornings with no motivation to even go to work because you're utterly miserable. The first step you can take to learning how to handle this, is to understand the reasons behind your micromanager's behavior. Once you've got that down, here's what else you can do:

Understand why they micromanage and then see what you can do to change it—They may be under an enormous amount of stress, trusted employees in the past who failed them, or perhaps it's literally just who they are. Continuing to the next step depends on the reason why they micromanage because there's little you can do when it's something like their personality. If it's something you can influence, now you find ways to build trust or even try to help them overcome whatever is making them act that way towards their team.

Build trust—A relationship without trust is a waste of time and meaningless; this is true in love, friendship, and work. Simply wanting your boss to stop micromanaging you will never work if you haven't won their trust and proven that they can calmly hand tasks over to you as well as provide you with the freedom to make decisions independently. Easier said than done? I know, but that's the thing with trust—it's tough to build and easy to lose. Try demonstrating that you can be trusted with a task by producing exceptional work and frequently communicate your progress. Building a personal relationship in the workplace often helps establish and improve trust.

Share your feelings by starting a discussion—Yes, I know, it may seem frightening or absurd but believe me, it's only at first. This is one of the most direct ways to deal with a micromanager—start a discussion about how their management affects you. Tell them if it's negatively impacting your performance and general workflow. This doesn't mean bite their head off or challenge their competency. Honestly, politely, and calmly explain how what they're doing is making you doubt your abilities and how it's making you dread coming to work. Be sure to not let anger overcome you and avoid being defensive as it may defeat the purpose of the discussion.

Set realistic expectations and healthy boundaries—This may have to fall into the same conversation above. Be sure to establish what is expected of you and what you're responsible for as well as the expectations and responsibilities of your manager so that there's no room for misunderstanding in the work process. After setting boundaries, don't be afraid to let your manager know when they're crossing them. I understand this too may be frightening but as long as these things are communicated in a polite and professional manner, they can be lessons learned and it could do wonders for the condition in the workspace.

Be consistent in communication and two-way feedback—Now that you've done all the above, don't think that it ends here. This is an ongoing process that can't be changed overnight, so you should do your best to constantly keep up the communication and two-way feedback. This is to prevent things from changing for a short while and then returning back to normal. Remain steadfast in your above actions and speak to your manager to ensure that they are satisfied with what you are producing.

These may all seem like you'll never be able to get through to such an "obsessive control-freak," but remember that they're only human, and that means that there's room for reason. Sitting and hating your job is not going to do you any favors so don't be afraid to be proactive as you may be doing these things to improve your own working environment but you may very well be helping your micromanager take their first steps toward servant leadership too.

Chapter 8

Certainty in Times of Uncertainty

The advice shared with us by Rudyard Kipling in his poem *If*, was and continues to be a great source of guidance on how one should live one's life—through challenges and adversity. The particular line I'd like to draw your attention to is, "If you can keep your head when all about you are losing theirs and blaming it on you," and the reason for my emphasis on this sentence is because of how accurately it represents one of the biggest challenges great leaders need to learn to manage.

Favorable conditions make it easy for many leaders to flourish and prosper in their roles because when the ship sails through calm waters, there's rarely any need to look to the leader for urgent and critical decisions. It's only when the ship encounters a storm that the crew frantically request the leader's guidance and expect the leader to steer them safely through the uncertainty.

What many don't realize; however, is that the calmness placed the leader at a disadvantage since many of them are caught unprepared when they're required to navigate significant changes and sudden pressure. The leaders who are prepared, will not only survive, but grow and excel.

The Covid-19 pandemic has arguably been one of the most uncertain times for the global workforce—spanning practically 3-years long with many of us not knowing how long we'll still have our jobs nor what the future holds for our companies. Almost every single business across the world has had to make significant alterations to their work processes, workflow, employee management, among other things. Not to mention the uncertainty of when or if things would ever go back to normal. We had no choice but to ride the storm and see where it takes us, then pick up the pieces from there.

Thankfully, we didn't have to do this alone. Companies were able to gather leaders who had the capacity to lead as agents of certainty amidst uncertain times. While the pandemic and its major effects have slowed down, companies are still trying to establish ways to recover and hopefully better handle any similar economic devastations in the future—this why they're now looking back at the qualities of the great leaders which saved their business as well as their employees, because this is what's needed in such uncertain times.

Below are 3 of the many traits a great leader in uncertain times, possesses:

- **Mindfulness**: This characteristic is certainly one that pops up a lot when discussing the qualities of great leaders, regardless of the circumstances. Why is that? Well, in this case, it's because a leader in uncertain times understands that there's not much guarantee in an uncertain future. They know how important it is to learn from the past, but they never fail to acknowledge that this doesn't mean we can change it. Uncertain times are what great leaders use as ways to help them focus on what can be done in the present to be better prepared for uncertainty in the future as well as how what they've learnt can be used to devise a strategy for a successful future.

- **Foundation**: Great leaders tend to have a flexible foundation in place as well as a terrific team with exceptional teamwork capabilities. They particularly mold their team to be versatile so that they wouldn't fall apart when change is implemented. They also build flexible teams in order to draw out the best of the team's abilities and stimulate out-of-the-box thinking, so that, in times of difficulty, they may be able to come up with and share ideas the leader may have overlooked.

- **Consistency**: Leaders who create consistency in the workplace reduces uncertainty in uncertain times. A consistent workforce requires 3 basic things: Collective understanding of team goals, a supportive, learning environment where everyone is equipped with the necessary tools and feel valued, and steadfastness in their winning strategy. Quality, training, and positive work ethics are essential for the success of the whole company.

A great leader is one who is able to keep their head in the game even while staring uncertainty right in the face. This means preventing uncertainty from creating even more uncertainty.

Strategies for Leading Through Uncertainty

We've always known how important a leader's ability to navigate disruption, change, and uncertainty is, but nothing made that clearer than the pandemic. We may hope and try to avoid future pandemics but who knows what'll hit us next. We cannot escape ever-increasing complexity.

Many leaders often deal with a rollercoaster of emotions like feeling ill-equipped, stuck, or overwhelmed as they're faced with the growing challenges of their roles. This is completely understandable especially when we're met with situations where the complexity of our world surpasses our comprehension. An easier description of what this means is using computing power as an example, though it has increased more than a trillion-fold since its introduction to the world, the human brain has remained the same.

This is where learning to lead oneself becomes the first step in effectively leading others in increasing complexity. While each leader will face their own particular circumstances, there are 6 strategies that have been found to accelerate a leader's ability to continuously evolve, learn, and navigate new and more complex challenges.

These are:

- **Distinguishing between complex and complicated**—These two terms are usually used interchangeably, though they represent gravely different circumstances. For instance, tax laws are complicated which means it's highly technical in nature and tough to understand but with the help of experts and breaking down the problem into careful parts, finding solutions is generally easier. Whereas with complex challenges, there are significantly more interdependent elements, many of which may be unknown and may possibly change over time—often in ways we cannot predict. Additionally, changes or actions in one dimension may result in unforeseen and disproportionate outcomes. Examples of complex challenges are climate change or foreign policies. Though these topics may not be lacking in hypothesis, guaranteed solutions are still unclear. This means that the solutions to complex challenges typically involve trial and error, and require a considerable amount of humility, willingness, and the ability to adapt, act, and learn.

- **Letting go of perfectionism**—Because complex situations and environments continuously change, aiming for perfection is pointless. Leaders should instead aim for continuous progress while still expecting mistakes. You should also keep in mind that as the course changes, you have the capacity to evaluate your options and correct the course where and as needed. High-achievers may find that their need for perfection, their ego, and desired identities, could get in their way of successfully letting go of this inherent need. We can only let go of perfectionism once we identify and acknowledge the core fears that trigger this need. The underlying or unexpressed fears behind this need may be that we feel we may not recover from mistakes or failure. Talking to others whom you respect about failures or mistakes in your role may be a great way to help you see that new opportunities, learning, and professional growth can or has been the result of such failures. It rarely results in catastrophes that could end their career, which is generally what is imagined to be the outcome. If you loosen the grip of these assumptions, over time, you'll find yourself more capable and comfortable letting go of perfectionism.

- **Embracing the unease of not knowing**—The time spent in our roles of leadership has conditioned us to come up with solutions; meaning straightforward, definitive, accurate answers and because our brains are wired to perceive uncertainty as a risk or a threat to the business, it's normal to feel stress or pressure when faced with daunting, unfamiliar situations— particularly for high-achievers who have built their careers on readily knowing or finding the perfect solutions. This makes us more inclined to try to avoid these unpleasant feelings but they tend to hinder our learning, personal growth, and overall performance. Instead of trying to avoid these feelings, we should learn to welcome unease and discomfort as a normal and expected part of the learning process. The CEO of Microsoft, Satya Nadella, perfectly explains how leaders should shift their mindsets from "knowing it all", to "learning it all." This shift will help leaders welcome discomfort and remove some of the pressure to have all the answers.

- **Resisting quick fixes**—When complex challenges seem too daunting, we may be tempted to oversimplify them so they don't intimidate us as much. An example of this is breaking a challenge into its respective components. While it may help you feel like you've got a greater command of the challenge, it may also narrow your view and lead to a false sense of security. Furthermore, drawing similarities from challenges you've faced in the past can also be useful but it may also lead you to overlook unique nuances of the present challenge. It's typical for high-achievers to be easily frustrated by challenges that don't present obvious solutions, or a clear course of action—this makes them more susceptible to giving in to the desire for quick resolution. Leaders should instead learn to balance their desire for action with a disciplined approach to understanding the core problem.

- **Zooming Out**—Excessive immersion in a challenge prevents a leader from "zooming out," or taking a step back to gain a different perspective of the matter at hand. Allowing yourself to zoom out helps you obtain a systematic view of the issues and can help you notice unexamined assumptions which may have gone unnoticed otherwise. Interdependencies and more critical patterns become more observable from this vantage point which automatically reveals new solutions and make calculating unforeseen obstacles easier. This is what's considered a more holistic perspective and it allows for improved adaptability and course correction. When you make this a regular practice, you build your capacity to see the bigger picture and improve your agility. We as leaders need to be reminded that we cannot control the uncertainty, the extent of change, or complexity we face. This doesn't mean we shouldn't do our utmost to adopt the strategies we need to improve our capacity to continually grow, learn, and better navigate the increasing complexities the world may throw at us.

- **Avoid doing it alone**—Believe it or not, may leaders fall victim to feelings of overwhelming isolation during challenging, uncertain times. This is mainly as a result of the implicit belief that leaders need to resolve all issues by themselves. When we witness workloads increasing in volume and complexity, we become inclined to increase our individual efforts and double-down on our focus. This strategy may be perfectly effective in the case of short-term challenges with more conspicuous solutions; however, in the case of challenges where there are not only unclear solutions, but also various interdependencies, this strategy may do more damage than good. These kinds of challenges should be used as a means to encourage leaders to intentionally reach out to their team, network, or beyond, for assistance—as to receive fresh, new insight, expertise and perspective. We need to accept that we all have limits to our knowledge and capacity for objective perspective on any or all situations. This doesn't mean that we can't exponentially expand our knowledge and capacities, but this cannot be accomplished without connecting with our peers and colleagues. With each one possessing their own set of expertise and perspectives, connecting with them will help us acquire the knowledge we need to tackle unfamiliar challenges—and in doing so, we promote our own learning, growth, and hopefully set an example for our subordinates. Remember that vulnerability comes with greater respect from your followers and your team will then be able to see just how much you value their experience and insight. Asking for the opinions of your various colleagues doesn't mean they need to offer you a solution, it simply opens the gateway for you to see things from a different viewpoint and possibly tap into unknown resources.

Common Mistakes Leaders Make When Facing a Crisis

The global pandemic has left organizations as well as their leaders at breaking point–the manner by which they handle crises has the potential to either make or break the business which is why many leaders are filled with fear and unease. The amount of knowledge is limited and the pace at which changes are taking place, are becoming increasingly hard to keep up with. According to corporate leadership advisor and author of *Future Shaper: how leaders can take charge in an uncertain world*, Niamh O'Keeffe, instead of becoming overwhelmed by the rise of new challenges, we should rewrite the rules to shape a better future for us as leaders and our organizations.

The way to shape a better future is to avoid or stop making the following mistakes (O'Keefe, 2020):

1. **Attempting to control the situation**: As leaders, we can all attest to the unfortunate reality that no rulebook could prepare us for a crisis like Covid-19. This means there may

be various other future challenges that nullify all that we've learnt. Obsessing over trying to gain control of such situations or allowing yourself to become overwhelmed by the lack of control is counterproductive and clouds your judgment. Rather shift your focus to the development of a new leadership skill: The ability to swiftly analyze an evolving situation and react with creativity, compassion, and collaborative solutions. We call this unchartered territory. The closest experience leaders faced that had similar detrimental characteristics would be the most recent global economic recession—we've also seen how leaders and government officials tapped into the lessons learned in those times to improve their resilience and devise temporary solutions. Uncertain times can be used as lessons to learn from and blueprints to help improve our contingency plans.

2. **Failing to step back and see the bigger picture**: What we witnessed with the Covid-19 pandemic was that many people placed enormous amounts of pressure on governments to exit lockdowns and assist the economy in getting back to "normal." The emphasis on "normal," however, implied that we falsely believed that things could go back to the way they were previously. Unfortunately, we later learned that task would not be as simple as we thought, since leaders were required to step back and look at the bigger picture. Getting everyone back on track required leaders to acknowledge the severity of short-term and long-term business economic fallout caused by the pandemic—they were responsible for pivoting businesses accordingly which meant adjusting or creating new products, services, and service platforms (among other things). Failure to step back and look at the bigger picture hinders our chances

of successfully bringing our employees and business out of moments of great despair and financial loss.

3. **Lack of communication**: Moments of crisis call on our abilities to effectively and frequently communicate because people desperately want more information and reassurance than usual. To effectively communicate and remain consistent in your communication, set out how often you plan to provide updates and feedback, and be sure to stick to it. Don't allow a full week to pass and your employees and stakeholders are still awaiting communication from you—this generally results in a vacuum of silence that is inevitably filled with inaccurate, unhelpful fear-driven rumors. Don't become the kind of leader who cancels scheduled communication events, even in times that you don't have anything new to share. Stick to the planned communication session and inform your team that there's nothing new to communicate as yet. You may even want to use this time to encourage them and explain the plans you've put in place to continue working on finding solutions.

4. **Lack of transparency**: This basically involves the failure to inform customers or stakeholders of your plans to continue your operations—whether remotely or otherwise. Your customers need to know what you are doing to remain productive and that your team's commitment has not suffered as a result of whatever challenge you're facing. Working with customers in such a transparent way creates a bond of trust and they are left with the confidence that you and your team will manage to pull through. No-one enjoys being left in the dark and transparency will always trump secrecy as it shows your business has integrity and that you value your customers enough to share challenges with them(to a certain degree).

These are only some of the common mistakes leaders are making and require immediate attention, if we want to improve the way we run our business and manage our employees. It may be tough to implement at first but practicing mindfulness will help us get into the ideal habits of leadership.

Chapter 9

Inclusive Leadership

It truly is quite astonishing how people have failed to change even throughout thousands of years of civilization. Sure, we make technological advancements and even increase our knowledge yet we still have the same emotions, social perceptions, and motivations. This makes it even more mind boggling why leaders in today's age don't extract from thousands of years of knowledge to fully perfect their skills.

Let's have a look at the legendary round table of folklore's King Arthur. Him and his knights were strategically seated at a round table to prevent the possibility of claiming precedence over one another. Everyone at the round table were equal—this included King Arthur himself. This is precisely what I want to talk about next: Inclusive Leadership. King Arthur himself knew that this was an extremely effective form of leadership; the choice to make a seat, not simply a place for everyone at the table.

If we decode the last statement, what would we find? That a place for everyone at the table refers to everyone having a place to sit, whereas a seat at the table refers to having an esteemed position at the table, and all who are seated are given priority when they speak. An inclusive leader's responsibility is to give their employees a seat at the table, not just a place to sit.

This act is an exceptional form of leadership and enables each individual in your team to have a voice—whether one is a janitor and another an executive, anyone and everyone can have good ideas and all input should be valued. Companies grow and learn to respect employees when inclusive leadership is adopted. Inclusive leadership is the literal opening of your door to all your employees and the cultivation of an atmosphere where every single worker knows and feels that they are valued and heard and as such are motivated to perform outstandingly.

Below are some ways you can create inclusivity in your office:

- **Eliminate judgment**—allow yourself to be open to people's criticism, thoughts and ideas. Even if you think the idea may be a bit too "out-of-the-box," discussing and being open to hearing it, doesn't obligate action, it only shows your employees that you're willing to listen to their ideas as opposed to just shooting them down.

- **Introduce round table discussions**—of course this doesn't necessarily mean go out and get a round table, it's the concept that's the point here. Allow everyone equal opportunity to speak and present ideas. Furthermore, round table discussions mean that the leader's opinions, questions and feedback about the ideas being pitched, are the only ones that matter. Everyone is part of the discussion and their opinions and feedback are equally as important as that of the leader.

- **Implement growth discussions**—growth discussions eliminate room for criticism. Every idea is genuinely considered, questions are asked, and additional thoughts are presented as a means to try and grow the presented idea. If the idea still doesn't end up seeming feasible, at least it was given a fair chance of consideration, analysis and evaluation.

- **Encourage positive responses**—An inclusive leader prioritizes the establishment of an atmosphere of praise. Thank all your employees for their input and encourage continued involvement and participation.

- **Take notes**–it doesn't have to be you but make sure that notes are being taken during these meetings and you're not just hosting a hypothetical chat. You've gathered your team to discuss ideas, right? So, it's needless to say that someone should be assigned to write them all down. This is a clear indication to your employees that their participation is being taken seriously. If you bring them all together and don't even bother with somehow recording what they have to say, it all just seems like meaningless effort.

- **Follow up on ideas**–Regardless of whether or not an idea will be moved forward, it's important that you follow up with all employees who were involved. Thank them honestly and open your conversation for additional participation.

Successful leaders have no issue with being inclusive leaders and offering their entire team a seat at the table. Every idea, no matter how peculiar, is valuable; even simply as a tool to help build a better relationship with the leader and employee.

Why Is Inclusive Leadership Important?

An inclusive workplace sets a tone that shows all employees that their differences are not frowned upon or rejected but rather welcomed and valued. Their unique points of view are encouraged and their individuality revered. The unfortunate reality, however, is that not every company is as inclusive as they would like to believe. One in four employees actually feel like they don't belong in their particular workplace, which in turn means that they're unable to bring their complete, authentic selves to work (Personio, 2021). The only way we can change this is by making systematic changes and leadership is where it starts.

What Is Inclusive Leadership?

Inclusive leadership refers to a management styled aimed at eliminated discrimination, bias, and favoritism. Inclusive leaders respect and value each individual's unique point of view, opinion, and background irrespective of their protected characteristics, which include:

- Language
- Nationality
- Sexual Orientation
- Ethnicity
- Gender
- Religion
- Culture
- Race
- Education
- Socio-Economic Status

- – Physical Or Mental Disability
- – Age
- – Race
- – Color

Qualities of Inclusive Leaders

Inclusive leadership requires continual learning and unlearning as it is an ongoing practice. It also involves perfecting several important qualities, some of which may come naturally to the leaders of your organization and some may not. Whichever way, it's important that an inclusive leader adapts and adopts these qualities, perfects them over time, and passes on these skills and knowledge to their fellow leaders and subordinates.

These qualities are:

Self-Awareness

Inclusive leaders know what their own biases are and work tirelessly to overcome them to prevent them from affecting their leadership. They are also the ones who implement systems and processes in a business that help reduce bias, so as to even the playing field for everyone.

Exceptional Communication

All inclusive leaders understand the importance of excellent communication. They also know that this involves a balance of talking and listening. They have the ability to take in information without judging the person speaking to them, they respond with empathy, they don't make hasty or rash decisions, and consider their words carefully.

Open-Mindedness

These leaders additionally have the ability to consider different perspectives in a situation and act without prejudice. Their natural curiosity means they have a passion for learning and crave gaining insight into beliefs and backgrounds that differ from their own. Furthermore, they are aware of the fact that they don't hold all the answers to all life's problems and have no issues with showing humility rather than pride. Inclusive leaders have a tendency to ask questions to fill the gaps in their own knowledge and open the floor for subject matter experts to share critical information.

Commitment

As with many good leaders, inclusive leaders understand that one must be the change one wishes to see so they take on that personal responsibility by continuously learning, demonstrating, and sharing what it means to be welcoming and inclusive. They're committed to investing the energy, time, and resources needed to develop the best possible environment for their workers.

Team Spirit

Inclusive are not only in it for themselves. They have full faith in the power of inclusivity and how it can benefit their team, their own success, and the business as a whole.

Courage

They fearlessly support their team members, particularly those belonging to minority groups or marginalized communities. Inclusive leaders have no fear standing up to detrimental or outdated beliefs in their organization, and they firmly hold others accountable for encouraging such beliefs—no matter their status within the company.

Cultural Intelligence

They have a vast knowledge and understanding of cultural norms and have the ability to adapt their communication style and behavior to each unique scenario. Inclusive leaders have exceptional self-awareness that makes it possible for them to understand how their own culture has influenced and conditioned their behavior and perspectives as well as the biases it may have instilled in them.

How Inclusive Leadership Can Help Your Business

Believe it or not, inclusivity is about much more than simply fostering positive emotions. It can have legitimate, measurable impacts on your business. Employees experience 3.4 times more job satisfaction and 2.7 times increased commitment to the business when managers are viewed as inclusive (Personio, 2021).

Take these 5 unexpected benefits of inclusive leadership into consideration, and then ask yourself why you haven't implanted this in your own company yet:

- **Elevated creativity**: Each employee brings with them a plethora of skills, ideas, and unique experiences to work with them daily; however, if you've failed to create an inclusive environment that makes it possible for them to freely share and explore those ideas, I'm afraid you're missing out. Inclusive environment eliminates the harboring of feelings that one doesn't belong and promotes psychological safety that emboldens employees to voice their opinions freely. This is where you as a leader can benefit because those opinions could be potential ideas and possibly lead to a whole new realm of innovation and creativity. You miss out on this opportunity if your employees are worried that their opinions may be rejected or misunderstood and so choose to remain silent and uninvolved.

- **Amplified performance**: Employees who feel included and filled with the sense that their company is committed to diversity, have reported improved innovative performance and more positive responses to customer needs. Gender diversity has also proven to be quite beneficial since companies with 30% of its executives consisting of females have been found to outperform companies where there is less gender diversity in executive roles (Personio, 2021).

- **Welcoming and positive culture**: Once again leading by example comes into play. Leaders who prioritize and exhibit inclusivity, often unwittingly, encourage their team to mimic this behavior. Sometimes they do it more outright and make it clear as day that discrimination and bias have no place in their company. They also know how to utilize positive reinforcement to stimulate and encourage participation.

- **Increase in company talent**: A remarkable 76% of jobseekers have confirmed that a diverse workforce is a key factor in evaluating job offers and companies to work for (Personio, 2021). It's evident that the workers in today's age are after more than a mere paycheck—they want to work for employers who not only operate through inclusivity but are also not afraid to voice their beliefs in equality.

- **Reduced staff turnover**: People hope to see themselves represented in a business's leadership team. This inspires them and shows them that reaching higher ranks in the company is not impossible and it further confirms that their success will not be determined or hampered by their gender, race, or any other protected characteristic. Employees who feel underrepresented, included, valued, or supported tend to leave the business quickly—especially if they are already part of underrepresented communities or minority groups.

Chapter 10

Empowered Leadership

The days when supervisors and management used to stand over an employee's shoulder, breathing down their neck, pushing them to work hard, are long gone. There has been a significant increase in recent years to establish and perfect the practice of empowered leadership.

Empowered leaders have the exceptional knack of getting the most out of their employees while at the same reducing the amount of stress on their employees. They understand that efficiency comes from the higher ranks and I'm not trying to say that being an efficient leader means your employees will automatically be efficient too. Though this is not impossible, it's not what I'm saying. What is meant by efficiency comes from the higher ranks is that an empowered leader equips their team with the tools, support systems, and trains their workforce on how to work as a team.

How to Make Employees Comfortable in Uncomfortability

As an empowered leader, be ready to have your leadership effort challenged from time to time. No, I'm not referring to a troublesome and challenging employee or one single situation. What I'm referring to is a legitimate challenge such as the uncertainty of your organization being bought by another. We're talking substantial payoff or product releases with notable defects.

It's easy to have all the confidence in our leadership skills when the world is operating smoothly and we face little to no challenges; however, the moments that define our skills as empowered leaders are the times of struggle and hardship. To keep your company operating at its best amidst difficult times, requires you to help your team stay at their best, and how can this be done? By helping them feel comfortable.

Here are some ways you can help your employees feel comfortable in uncomfortability:

- **Offer privacy.** You may be hanging around with a positive disposition but the truth is not everyone enjoys it when their leader hangs around. Even if you're being supportive, you may seem as though you're hovering too much. Your employees need the freedom to work on their own, so be open to giving this to them. This doesn't go for everyone as some may need this more than others, but try to look out for any cues.
- **Promote open communication.** This one may be on the list a few times but it's to emphasize its importance. Open communication is a way of building trust with employees and additionally shows that you care. Be open to suggestions for improvement or be willing to lend an ear to an employee who

simply needs to talk. As with most things in life, communication is the key to success.

- **Erect a location for anonymous suggestions**. After doing so, don't let the suggestions gather dust; actively and frequently review these suggestions. You may find some truly life-changing recommendations in there that you wished you'd thought about, an added plus is to praise those suggestions publicly. Though you don't know whose suggestions they are, the relevant person will feel valued and you will be reducing the common fear of criticism. This may also encourage other employees to be more responsive to offering ideas of their own.

- **Regularly praise employees**. You don't have to keep showering them with endless gifts and adoration but be sure to openly show your appreciation of their efforts. They need to know that their hard work does not go unnoticed and this is another way of keeping their morale high. It may also push other employees to want to work hard so that they too can experience the pleasure of praise.

- **Where possible, adapt a homestyle workplace**. No, I'm not saying allow people to come dressed in pajamas and blankets. A homestyle workplace simply means providing comfort by bringing some of the elements of home to work. Monthly team lunches or picnics are a terrific way to bring employees together. Casual dress days and team buildings are also great to help them share their interests and hobbies.

In order to build a team that knows how to manage working in easy and challenging times, it's essential for leaders to help them feel comfortable in these uncomfortable situations. If you struggle to think of how to make this possible, take a moment to reflect on any uncomfortable periods in your work life and then think about what you wished you had received from your team or superiors that may have helped you feel more comfortable.

The idea of empowering the members of one's team has become quite the hot topic these days, and I can totally understand why. A good leader is characterized by their ability to empower others and achieve maximum success. In order to effectively introduce this in your organization, it's important that you thoroughly think through what "empowerment" means and how best to employ it in your organization in order to harness its strength. The definition of leadership, according to the US Army, contains inferred references to empowerment, "influencing people by providing purpose, direction, and motivation, while operating to accomplish the mission and improve the organization." (Huntoon, n.d.) Empowerment manages to do all of this.

What Is Empowered Leadership?

Empowerment requires the inclusion of the entire team in matters of decision-making as well as giving them participatory roles that capitalizes their own knowledge and expertise—increasing their sense of personal worth and their commitment to the company. Empowerment is also a demonstration of exceptional listening skills, and appreciation of the insight and input of everyone in your team. Empowering your team should be viewed as motivating them to "row together." This increases the overall success of your mission and builds confidence in their ability to execute your collective goals. It also cultivates trust in an organization and gives rise to a secondary level of leadership that may be necessary when you're not present for key decisions.

While empowerment sounds great in theory, it may not always be as simple since leadership is fundamentally about the human dimension.

Embracing empowered leadership may be tougher for some leaders to adopt because of personality contradictions—being placed in charge of a team or company may have some believing that their decisions and presence is the only thing responsible for the company's prosperity. The hard, long work they put in to get to the top may be the reason why these leaders feel that their decisions are what has led their company or team to success and increasing profits. This may be why they don't see the need to empower subordinates but this may be the very thing that either keeps their success stagnant or dramatically reduces it over time.

Empower Your Team

Well, the answers are crystal clear: Because no matter how educated, experienced, open-minded, or innovative you are, no one person has the capacity to lead an organization on their own. The success of a business relies on the collective excellence of many. Everyone is a leader based on the significant amount of work, time, and effort put in by each member of the team—they've contributed, labored, and committed to the same goals as ours so why should they not be empowered? The further you climb up the corporate ladder, the more dependent you become on the diverse skill sets and talents of those behind your company's ability to thrive. As leaders, part of our success is mentoring, coaching, and empowering those we serve. At some point in our leadership development, we have all been empowered by knowledgeable, enlightened seniors who saw the potential in us to lead at their level. They are the ones who gave us the opportunity to prove ourselves through taking on significant responsibilities, underwrote our mess-ups, and continued to shape and develop us for their roles in time. It is for this reason that empowering our teams starts with understanding the pool of collective excellence in every business that, as time passes, empowers the goal. We need to only remember the confidence and trust that was placed in us early in our own careers, who witnessed our potential, and allowed us the chance to fulfill such a promise.

Successful Businesses Empower Their Leadership

Empowerment is a magnificent tool used to create positive, healthy, and successful companies. This is a method whether there is no ownership of the vision and utter trust in the leadership. Listening to your subordinates, carefully and considerately acting on their inputs means you not only empower them but also your company. Your team takes greater responsibility and extra care when tasked with acting on your behalf in well-defined, key situations. They will also be confident that they understand and know your vision and intent and would be less likely to unwittingly deviate from this. You can be sure that they have thought thoroughly on what actions to take, with the collective goal and intent in mind. This means that being empowered is a way of building future leaders for your company or for whatever future prospects are in store for them.

You can take pride in knowing that not only were you taught and mentored by exceptional people to get where you are today, but you continued to learn, grow, and evolve for the benefit of yourself and your company, as well as the benefit of those whom you led. They will remember you in their future roles and how you stood beside them, welcoming all of what they had to offer without secretly pushing or disregarding them. This means that the future will consist of well-trained, empathetic, servant leaders who understand the importance of empowering others—and hopefully the cycle continues. Though this is a splendid way of motivating yourself to try this approach, ultimate credit shouldn't be the motivation behind your empowerment because it won't last very long nor will it take you very far. Your core reason for wanting to empower your team should be so that everyone who has a hand in your company and who crosses your path knows and understands their value and how important the contribution of the entire team is. If you fail to find this reason behind your motivation, then you may be facing a problem and need some further adjustments.

Conclusion

We've reached the end and hopefully learnt valuable qualities that'll assist us not only in our endeavors to become exceptional leaders but also throughout our lives–helping us to be exceptional people. My hope for each one of you is that you learn how to shift your focus from being your team's authority, to being your team's main resource and example.

The last advice I'd like to give you is the following

Empower People

Why and how should leaders do this? Well, this has basically been what the entire book was about. The act of empowering people isn't a casual act but rather a continuous and comprehensive process, in need of regular review to analyze its effectiveness. If you're still a bit two-minded on how this will even work and riddled with questions like: How would I even know the team is doing what's needed to accomplish your goals? How can you know for sure that they understand your intent? What if they are screwing up or moving in a direction they're not meant to go?

Good leaders empower but keep an eye on the effectiveness of this empowerment. You're not being asked to empower and then leave everything in everyone else's hands. This will only have you worried, uneasy, and overcome with stress. You can still successfully empower people and check its effectiveness. Take it from President Reagan understood this very well when he stated, "Trust, but verify."

We've seen that this is accomplishable through communicating our intent with our team and then encouraging them to contribute their recommendations and ideas to help improve the business. Listen to the recommendations you've asked for and incorporate the ideas that can be incorporated and then decide on a path forward. This in no way means you've sacrificing or surrendering your accountability and legal authority. You will still ultimately be the one held accountable should one of your team members be trusted with a big responsibility and make a significant error.

This is actually on of the fundamental principles of commanding an organization in the US Army. Before they are commissioned, they are taught that they are responsible for everything that either happens or fails to happen in their command. This principle can be applied to the concept for leader of companies too, no matter how big or small. You should regularly check to see if your team understand the mission, is following your intent, and is moving your company forward. Empowerment is something to be demonstrated, earned, and checked frequently. This can be done through a combination of measures like timeliness, effectiveness, and good listening—at no time; however, should this border micromanage.

Every leader's toolkit should eventually contain empowerment. It strengthens everyone within a company, keeps the company on the path to success, and builds the most significant element on any team—trust. Trust between leader and lead as well as trust between everyone on the team.

Empowerment invests in people and you'll soon come to find that there is no greater ROI in any profession.

References

Boss, J. (2017, June 27). *Lead Yourself First*. Forbes. https://www.forbes.com/sites/jeffboss/2017/06/27/lead-yourself-first/

Brown, D. S. N. (2022, July 22). *Leadership Vs. Management*. Digital First Magazine. https://www.digitalfirstmagazine.com/leadership-vs-management/

Brown, S. (2021, August 10). *Leading Self And Others*. Brainz. https://www.brainzmagazine.com/post/leading-self-and-others

Brown, S. (2021, November 1). *Leading – Not Lording Over*. Brainz Magazine. https://www.brainzmagazine.com/post/leading-not-lording-over

Brown, S. (2021, December 2). *Servant Leadership*. Brainz Magazine. https://www.brainzmagazine.com/post/servant-leadership

Brown, S. (2022, January 17). *How To Serve While You Lead – A Story*. Brainz Magazine. https://www.brainzmagazine.com/post/how-to-serve-while-you-lead-a-story

Brown, S. (2022, March 18). *Leadership – Being An Aspirin Inspite Of Your Migraine*. Brainz Magazine. https://www.brainzmagazine.com/post/leadership-being-an-aspirin-inspite-of-your-migraine

Brown, S. (2022, April 8). *Leadership – Certainty In Times Of Uncertainty*. Brainz Magazine. https://www.brainzmagazine.com/post/leadership-certainty-in-times-of-uncertainty

Brown, S. (2022, May 3). *Inclusive Leadership – Making A Seat, Not A Place For Everyone*. Brainz Magazine. https://www.brainzmagazine.com/post/inclusive-leadership-making-a-seat-not-a-place-for-everyone

Brown, S. (2022, July 6). *Empowered Leadership – Making People Feel Comfortable In Un-Comfortability*. Brainz Magazine. https://www.brainzmagazine.com/post/empowered-leadership-making-people-feel-comfortable-in-un-comfortability

Carucci, R. (2015, December 4). *Great Leaders Know They're Not Perfect*. Harvard Business Review. https://hbr.org/2015/12/great-leaders-know-theyre-not-perfect

Cole, M. (2019, January 11). *How Can You Serve and Lead at the Same Time?* John C. Maxwell. https://www.johnmaxwell.com/blog/mark-cole-how-can-you-serve-and-lead-at-the-same-time/

Conlow, R. (2021, May 24). *The 5 Greatest Servant Leaders of All-Time*. Rick Conlow International. https://rickconlow.com/5-greatest-servant-leaders-of-all-time/

Daskal, L. (n.d.). *12 Mistakes to Avoid As a First Time Leader*. Lolly Daskal. https://www.lollydaskal.com/leadership/12-mistakes-to-avoid-as-a-first-time-leader/

Eikenberry, K. (2009, May 15). *Five Ways to Serve Others as a Leader*. Social Media Today. https://www.socialmediatoday.com/content/five-ways-serve-others-leader

Forbes Coaches Council. (2020, March 9). *Council Post: 16 Ways Leaders Can Get Comfortable With Not Having All The Answers*. Forbes. https://www.forbes.com/sites/forbescoachescouncil/2020/03/09/16-ways-leaders-can-get-comfortable-with-not-having-all-the-answers/?sh=5f0627b27f89

How Successful Leaders Use Empowerment to Build Trust and Excellence. (n.d.). David Huntoon. https://www.davidhuntoon.

com/leaders/successful-leaders-use-empowerment-build-
trust-excellence/#:~:text=Defining%20Leadership%20
Empowerment&text=Empowering%20builds%20
confidence%20in%20their

Janzen, A. (2021, May 17). *How To Be A Servant Leader Without Burning Yourself Out.* Forbes. https://www.forbes.com/sites/
forbescoachescouncil/2021/05/17/how-to-be-a-servant-leader-
without-burning-yourself-out/?sh=57d796131e39

Kokemuller, N. (n.d.). *The X&Y Management Theory.* Chron. https://
smallbusiness.chron.com/xy-management-theory-55198.html

Neale, P. (2020, May 26). *Council Post: Why Servant Leadership Is More Important Than Ever.* Forbes. https://www.forbes.com/
sites/forbescoachescouncil/2020/05/26/why-servant-leadership-
is-more-important-than-ever/?sh=7ad00ec22861

O'Hara, C. (2018, July 5). *How to Manage an Employee Who's Having a Personal Crisis.* Harvard Business Review. https://hbr.org/2018/07/
how-to-manage-an-employee-whos-having-a-personal-crisis

O'Keefe, N. (2020, April 28). *7 Mistakes Leaders Often Make In a Crisis. Firsthand.* https://firsthand.co/blogs/workplace-issues/
7-leadership-mistakes

Painter, M. (2014, April 8). *Artificial Versus Authentic Leadership.* Association for Talent Development. https://www.td.org/
magazines/td-magazine/artificial-versus-authentic-leadership

Patel, O. H. (n.d.). *Origins of Servant Leadership.* Clearly Agile. https://
www.clearlyagile.com/agile-blog/origins-of-servant-leadership

Personio. (2021, December 30). *Why Inclusive Leadership Matters For Employees.* Personio. https://www.personio.com/blog/
inclusive-leadership/

Petrova, B. (2021, June 11). *What Is Micromanagement And How To Deal With It?* Slingshot. https://www.slingshotapp.io/blog/what-is-micromanagement

Van Slyke, C. (2016, June 30). *Purposefulness: One of the Four Pillars of Self-Leadership.* Flagstaff Business News. https://www.flagstaffbusinessnews.com/purposefulness-one-four-pillars-self-leadership/

Zucker, R., & Rowell, D. (2021, April 26). *6 Strategies for Leading Through Uncertainty.* Harvard Business Review. https://hbr.org/2021/04/6-strategies-for-leading-through-uncertainty

Printed in the United States
by Baker & Taylor Publisher Services